American Graffiti

Combining a detailed film analysis with archival research and social science approaches, this book examines how *American Graffiti* (1973), a low-budget and star-less teen comedy by a filmmaker whose only previous feature had been a box office flop, became one of the highest grossing and most highly acclaimed films of all time in the United States, and one of the key expressions of the nostalgia wave washing over the country in the 1970s.

American Graffiti: George Lucas, the New Hollywood and the Baby Boom Generation explores the origins and development of the film, its form and themes as well as its marketing, reception, audiences and impact. It does so by considering the life and career of the film's co-writer and director George Lucas; the development and impact of the baby boom generation to which he, many of his collaborators and the vast majority of the film's audience belonged; the transformation of the American film industry in the late 1960s and 1970s; and broader changes in American society which gave rise to an intense sense of crisis and growing pessimism across the population.

This book is ideal for students, scholars and those with an interest in youth cinema, the New Hollywood and George Lucas as well as both Film and American Studies more broadly.

Peter Krämer is a Senior Research Fellow in Cinema and TV at De Montfort University, Leicester, UK. He is the author or editor of 11 academic books, mainly about American film history and Hollywood's global dimensions.

Cinema and Youth Cultures

Series Editors: Siân Lincoln and Yannis Tzioumakis

Cinema and Youth Cultures engages with well-known youth films from American cinema as well as the cinemas of other countries. Using a variety of methodological and critical approaches, the series volumes provide informed accounts of how young people have been represented in film, while also exploring the ways in which young people engage with films made for and about them. In doing this, the Cinema and Youth Cultures series contributes to important and long-standing debates about youth cultures, how these are mobilized and articulated in influential film texts and the impact that these texts have had on popular culture at large.

Mustang
Translating Willful Youth
Elif Akçalı, Cüneyt Çakırlar, Özlem Güçlü

Mary Poppins
Radical Elevation in the 1960s
Leslie H. Abramson

The Outsiders
Adolescent Tenderness and Staying Gold
Ann M. Ciasullo

American Graffiti
George Lucas, the New Hollywood and the Baby Boom Generation
Peter Krämer

For more information about this series, please visit: https://www.routledge.com/Cinema-and-Youth-Cultures/book-series/CYC

American Graffiti

George Lucas, the New Hollywood and the Baby Boom Generation

Peter Krämer

Routledge
Taylor & Francis Group

LONDON AND NEW YORK

First published 2023
by Routledge
4 Park Square, Milton Park, Abingdon, Oxon OX14 4RN

and by Routledge
605 Third Avenue, New York, NY 10158

Routledge is an imprint of the Taylor & Francis Group, an informa business

British Library Cataloguing-in-Publication Data
A catalogue record for this book is available from the British Library

Library of Congress Cataloging-in-Publication Data
Names: Krämer, Peter, 1961– author.
Title: American graffiti : George Lucas, the New Hollywood and the
Baby Boom generation / Peter Krämer.
Description: Abingdon, Oxon ; New York : Routledge, 2023. |
Series: Cinema and youth cultures | Includes bibliographical
references and index. |
Identifiers: LCCN 2022055361 (print) | LCCN 2022055362 (ebook) |
ISBN 9781138681910 (hardback) | ISBN 9780367523060 (paperback) |
ISBN 9781315545509 (ebook)
Subjects: LCSH: American graffiti (Motion picture) | Motion
pictures—United States—History—20th century. | Motion
pictures—Social aspects—United States—History—20th century.
Classification: LCC PN1997.A3428 K73 2023 (print) | LCC PN1997.
A3428 (ebook) | DDC 791.43/72—dc23/eng/20221208
LC record available at https://lccn.loc.gov/2022055361
LC ebook record available at https://lccn.loc.gov/2022055362

ISBN: 978-1-138-68191-0 (hbk)
ISBN: 978-0-367-52306-0 (pbk)
ISBN: 978-1-315-54550-9 (ebk)

DOI: 10.4324/9781315545509

Typeset in Times New Roman
by codeMantra

Contents

Figures

Series Editors' Introduction

Despite the high visibility of youth films in the global media marketplace, especially since the 1980s when Conglomerate Hollywood realized that such films were not only strong box office performers but also the starting point for ancillary sales in other media markets as well as for franchise building, academic studies that focused specifically on such films were slow to materialize. Arguably, the most important factor behind academia's reluctance to engage with youth films was a (then) widespread perception within the Film and Media Studies communities that such films held little cultural value and significance, and therefore were not worthy of serious scholarly research and examination. Just like the young subjects they represented, whose interests and cultural practices have been routinely deemed transitional and transitory, so were the films that represented them perceived as fleeting and easily digestible, destined to be forgotten quickly, as soon as the next youth film arrived in cinema screens a week later.

Under these circumstances, and despite a small number of pioneering studies in the 1980s and early 1990s, the field of 'youth film studies' did not really start blossoming and attracting significant scholarly attention until the 2000s and in combination with similar developments in cognate areas such as 'girl studies'. However, because of the paucity of material in the previous decades, the majority of these new studies in the 2000s focused primarily on charting the field and therefore steered clear of long, in-depth examinations of youth films or were exemplified by edited collections that chose particular films to highlight certain issues to the detriment of others. In other words, despite providing often wonderfully rich accounts of youth cultures as these have been captured by key films, these studies could not have possibly dedicated sufficient space to engage with more than just a few key aspects of youth films.

In more recent (post-2010) years, a number of academic studies started delimiting their focus and therefore providing more space for in-depth examinations of key types of youth films, such as slasher films and biker films or examining youth films in particular historical periods. From that point on, it was a matter of time for the first publications that focused exclusively on key youth films from a number of perspectives to appear (*Mamma Mia! The Movie*, *Twilight* and *Dirty Dancing* are among the first films to receive this treatment). Conceived primarily as edited collections, these studies provided a multifaceted analysis of these films, focusing on such issues as the politics of representing youth, the stylistic and narrative choices that characterize these films and the extent to which they are representative of a youth cinema, the ways these films address their audiences, the ways youth audiences engage with these films, the films' industrial location and other relevant issues.

It is within this increasingly maturing and expanding academic environment that the **Cinema and Youth Cultures** volumes arrive, aiming to consolidate existing knowledge, provide new perspectives, apply innovative methodological approaches, offer sustained and in-depth analyses of key films and therefore become the 'go to' resource for students and scholars interested in theoretically informed, authoritative accounts of youth cultures in film. As editors, we have tried to be as inclusive as possible in our selection of key examples of youth films by commissioning volumes on films that span the history of cinema, including the silent film era; that portray contemporary youth cultures as well as ones associated with particular historical periods; that represent examples of mainstream and independent cinema; that originate in American cinema and the cinemas of other nations; that attracted significant critical attention and commercial success during their initial release; and that were 'rediscovered' after an unpromising initial critical reception. Together these volumes are going to advance youth film studies while also being able to offer extremely detailed examinations of films that are now considered significant contributions to cinema and our cultural life more broadly.

We hope readers will enjoy the series.

Siân Lincoln & Yannis Tzioumakis
Cinema & Youth Cultures Series Editors

Acknowledgements

The main inspiration for this book was a visit to Modesto, California, in 2008. The city was then celebrating the 35th anniversary of the release of *American Graffiti*, a film that *Star Wars* creator George Lucas had made about his home town. Having previously spoken at an event at Modesto Junior College commemorating the 30th anniversary of *Star Wars*, I was invited back to introduce an evening screening of *American Graffiti* at the downtown State Theatre (see Krämer 2008/2018). This came after a rich programme of day-time events, including, among other things, a classic car show, an exhibition of memorabilia, a rock 'n' roll and doo-wop concert as well as panel discussions with Wendy Lucas (one of George's sisters), members of the Faros car club (the model for the film's Pharaohs gang), local legend Gene Winfield (a custom car builder who, like George Lucas, had left town to work in the film industry), actress Candy Clark (*American Graffiti*'s Debbie) and celebrated cinematographer Haskell Wexler (one of Lucas's early mentors).

I had always loved *American Graffiti*, but it was only on this day that it came truly alive for me, because for the first time I got a strong sense of the historical reality behind the film, both the reality of its difficult production in the early 1970s and the reality of the place and period it portrays – Modesto in the early 1960s. My greatest gratitude, therefore, goes to Richard Ravalli, who invited me to Modesto and was a generous host, going on to share his extensive knowledge about George Lucas with me. I also wish to thank Oliver Gruner, Jim Russell, Yannis Tzioumakis and Jim Whalley for involving me in some of their projects which turned out to be of great relevance for my work on this book, and for providing me with various research materials. Yannis deserves special thanks for his patience, guidance (especially when it came to shortening an excessively long manuscript) and support.

Introduction

Between 1970 and 1977, George Lucas developed and completed two films about teenagers which, to almost everyone's surprise, became huge box office hits and exerted an enormous influence on the surrounding culture. The impact of the first of these films – *American Graffiti* (1973) – was mainly confined to the United States, while the impact of the second – *Star Wars* (1977) – could, and still can, be felt around the world.

Lucas was only in his mid twenties when he started working on these two projects after his first feature *THX 1138* (1971), a highly stylised Science Fiction movie depicting a hyper-conformist underground society in which all people are subjected to enforced drug use and total surveillance so as to ensure their participation in pointless rituals of production and consumption, was deemed uncommercial by Warner Bros., the Hollywood studio that had funded its production. Warner Bros. executives responded very negatively to in-house screenings of the film in May and November 1970, their judgment being confirmed by the film's financially unsuccessful theatrical release in March 1971 (Jones 2016: 118–26; Taylor 2016: 100–4).[1]

Apart from *THX 1138* – which is more reminiscent of European art cinema and avant-garde works than of typical Hollywood productions – Lucas had only made documentaries and experimental movies up to this point, first as a film student and then as a freelancer.[2] His productions ranged from his film school debut *Look at Life* (1965) – a one-minute montage of often violent or sexualised still images from *Life* magazine – and a 24-minute documentary about a Los Angeles disc jockey and his youthful listeners (*The Emperor*, 1967) to a one-hour film about the making of Francis Ford Coppola's 1969 feature *The Rain People* (*filmmaker: a diary by George Lucas,* 1968). They also included the 15-minute film *THX 1138: 4EB* (1967) on which his first feature was based (Jones 2016: 52–96; Taylor 2016: 59–67, 90–100).

DOI: 10.4324/9781315545509-1

Lucas felt that, if he wanted to continue working as a movie director in control of his own projects, he needed a very commercial follow-up to his first feature, and he was determined to develop his own story for this, rather than accepting one of the directorial assignments (for other people's scripts) that he was offered (Jones 2016: 137; Taylor 2016: 109).

For inspiration, he turned to his own past, growing up in Modesto, a small town in Northern California. From his early years, he remembered the fascination and excitement of watching Science Fiction movie serials like *Flash Gordon* (Universal, 1936–40) on television and wondered whether it might be possible to produce an updated version of such adventures (Jones 2016: 130–1; Taylor 2016: 102–3). From his later teenage years, he recalled the importance of music, cars, sex and romance, and the necessity to make decisions about the future, as well as many teen movies dealing with these topics. He thought that this might provide him with good material for a semi-autobiographical film about teenagers (Jones 2016: 131–2; Taylor 2016: 103–4). In addition, he had been working, together with John Milius, on a project about the Vietnam war entitled *Apocalypse Now*, but this was unlikely to be considered a commercially attractive project at this time (Jones 2016: 101, 109, 127–30; Taylor 2016: 97, 101–2, 108).

It soon became clear that Lucas's second feature would be his teen movie, yet initial work on what was to become *Star Wars* ran parallel to the making and release of *American Graffiti*, with the Science Fiction story's focus eventually shifting from adult protagonists to teenagers Luke and Leia (Jones 2016: 130–90; Taylor 2016: 102–11, 124–39). Both projects were quite unusual: the comedy had multiple, complexly intertwined storylines accompanied by an almost continuous pop and rock radio soundtrack, and the space adventure included an extraordinarily complicated back story.

Lucas had a hard time finding studios willing to finance these projects. After initial funding from United Artists in 1971, he finally made a deal for *American Graffiti* with Universal in 1972 and shot the film in the San Francisco Bay Area, not that far from his home town (Jones 2016: 132–53; Taylor 2016: 103–11). Without *American Graffiti*'s commercial and critical success, it is unlikely that Lucas would have been able to sustain himself during the three and a half years in which his life was then focused on getting *Star Wars* made and to elicit sufficient studio support – from 20th Century-Fox – for the film's realisation (Jones 2016: 159–61, 167–239; Taylor 2016: 132–55, 173–98).

The success of *American Graffiti* was unprecedented for the kind of film it was. The story takes place in Modesto during one night at the end of the summer of 1962.[3] Mostly driving around town in cars, from dusk to dawn various young people have a series of particularly intense experiences – to do with sex and romance, friendship and rivalry, transgression and conformity, freedom and commitment, continuity and change – that force them to reflect on where they are at in their lives and, in several cases, to make important decisions about where they want to go with it. The film's actors were largely unknown, with the exception of Ron Howard – billed as Ronny Howard – who, among many other TV appearances, between the ages of 6 and 14 had been featured on *The Andy Griffith Show* (CBS), a top-rated sitcom running from 1960 to 1968,[4] and of Wolfman Jack, who played himself in *American Graffiti*. Legendary radio disc jockey Bob Smith had adopted the 'Wolfman Jack' persona in 1963, initially keeping his real identity a secret and broadcasting his show all across the United States from a high-powered Mexican border station; by 1973 he had become a no longer secretive multi-media celebrity.[5] Before *American Graffiti*, Wolfman Jack had only ever appeared in one movie (in a very small part).[6]

With a budget of $775,000, Lucas's film cost about a quarter of the average Hollywood movie released in 1973[7] and had one of the highest returns on investment in Hollywood history (cp. Block and Wilson 2010: 520). After its initial release by Universal in August 1973, *American Graffiti* stayed in movie theatres almost continuously until 1978. By the end of that year, it had earned a total of $55.9 million in domestic rentals, that is the distributor's share – usually around 50% – of exhibitors' revenues from ticket sales in the United States (Steinberg 1980: 5; the domestic box office take was $115 million).[8] In January 1979, *American Graffiti* was listed as the thirteenth highest-grossing movie of *all time* in the United States, and it was not that far from the top ten of an *inflation-adjusted* all-time chart compiled around the same time (Steinberg 1980: 3–5).[9] Almost all the other films close to the top of these two all-time charts, including *Star Wars* (at number 2 behind *Gone With the Wind* [Fleming, 1939] in the inflation-adjusted chart, and far ahead of the competition at number 1 in the non-adjusted chart), were big-budget productions and/or adaptations of stories previously successful in another medium (print or stage), and/or they featured major stars – whereas *American Graffiti* was a low-budget production without movie stars, based on an original screenplay.

In addition to the film's outstanding commercial success, *American Graffiti* was a critical hit with reviewers as well as with the Academy of Motion Picture Arts and Science and other organisations (Steinberg 1980: 248–9, 263, 270, 296). It was soon recognised as a classic. A survey of twenty leading film critics carried out in 1978 found that

American Graffiti was regarded as one of the very best American films of the preceding decade 1968–77 (156–68). And *Time* magazine declared *American Graffiti* to be one of the ten best films of the 1970s (178). Since then *American Graffiti* has come to be celebrated as one of the greatest American films of all time. It was selected by the National Film Preservation Board in 1995 and made it onto the American Film Institute's list of the 100 best American movies in 1997 (at number 77) and 2007 (no. 62) (Block and Wilson 2010: 558).

What is more, as a comedy set in 1962 about young people who are at high school or have just graduated from it (two of them on their way to college), *American Graffiti* paved the way for the success of two films ranking very highly in the non-adjusted all-time box office chart from January 1979: *National Lampoon's Animal House* (Landis, 1978; at number 15), another comedy set in 1962, this time at a university, and *Grease* (Kleiser, 1978, no. 4), a musical comedy about high school students in the late 1950s. In addition, Lucas's film was linked to two sitcoms that were among the ten top rated shows on American television from 1975 to 1979: *Happy Days* (CBS, 1974–84), which featured Ron Howard as a high-school student in the late 1950s, and its spin-off *Laverne & Shirley* (CBS, 1976–81), which co-starred Cindy Williams, another one of the leads in Lucas's film. Thus, *American Graffiti* was closely tied to an important trend in American popular culture of the 1970s, especially the second half of the decade. Often described as 'nostalgic', much of this popular culture cast an affectionate look back on the life of young people in the late 1950s and early 1960s.

George Lucas and the Baby Boom Generation

American Graffiti's original poster [see **frontispiece of this book**] features a drawing of teenagers hugging, dancing, kissing, driving and just hanging out, their hairdos and clothes evoking the fashion of the 1950s. The drawing shows the commercial culture these teenagers are immersed in, the products and services their leisure pursuits rely on: a Coca-Cola glass and a cheeseburger, a band and musical notation indicating the song it plays, flashy cars as well as places of amusement and consumption – a movie theatre showing *The Blob* (Yeaworth, 1958) and a restaurant from the famous Mel's Drive-In chain. For this drawing, cartoonist Mort Drucker used the exaggerated style of the television and movie parodies he had been doing for *Mad* magazine since the mid 1950s.[10] In terms of both content and style, then, the drawing evokes the past, as does the poster's tagline, prominently displayed just below the film's title: 'Where were you in '62?'

This tagline is spoken by Wolfman Jack at the very beginning and the very end of *American Graffiti*'s trailer,[11] which has the same kind of content as the poster, and also features plenty of funny dialogue, juvenile delinquents, various pranks, shots being fired, a car race as well as both minor and major car accidents. To the accompaniment of classic rock 'n' roll and pop songs, the trailer introduces the main characters by combining pages from a high-school yearbook with scenes from the film, highlighting their search for sex, love and recognition and the fact that important changes lie ahead of them; in the words of one of the characters: 'You can't stay seventeen forever'.

Complementing shots of cars driving around town at night, a male voiceover narrator demands: 'Grab that special one [...], cruise downtown and catch *American Graffiti*'. Viewers are invited to join the drivers in the trailer, the viewers' 1970s present being merged with the year 1962 depicted in the film: 'Go back in time!' Towards the end of the trailer, the narrator declares: 'It's one of those great old movies about romance, racing and rock 'n' roll'. *American Graffiti* was said to be as much a recreation of teen movies from the past as it was a depiction of teenagers' lives in the past.

Through their images, sounds and text, most importantly the tagline, poster and trailer invited those old enough in the prospective audience fondly to remember, and through the film perhaps to relive, their own past (including the teen movies they had seen), and to reflect on their country's recent history. The question 'Where were you in '62?' was uncomfortably, yet calculatedly, close to the oft-repeated claim that people remembered exactly where they were when they heard that President John F. Kennedy had been shot (in November 1963). Poster and trailer also strongly suggested that there was another major target audience in addition to the people who had been teenagers in 1962 – the teenagers of 1973. They could see a heightened version of their current lives on screen and directly engage with the decisions the teenagers in the film have to make: to leave home or to stay, to commit to a particular relationship or to dissolve it, to cling to certain aspects of their teen lives or to embrace growing up. By contrast, those who had been teenagers in 1962 could consider the friends they had kept or lost in the meantime, the places they had left behind or returned to and the paths they had taken or not taken in their lives.

Importantly, both groups belonged to the vast generational cohort known as the baby boom, that is people born during the years of exceptionally high birth rates between the mid 1940s and the mid 1960s.[12] In 1970, there were 77.2 million people aged 5–24 (that is, born between 1946 and 1965) in the United States, making up 38% of the American population (of 204.9 million people) at the time (Wattenberg 1976: 10). Given an average movie ticket price of just under $2 in 1973/74 (Steinberg 1980: 44), when *American Graffiti* earned most of its money at the box office, and a total gross from ticket sales of $115 million, the film sold almost 60 million tickets, which is not that far from matching the size of the baby boom generation. This suggests that most baby boomers saw *American Graffiti* and that the vast majority of the film's audience was made up of baby boomers.

Born on 14 May 1944 as the third, and last but one, child in a middle-class family, Lucas shared many of the defining generational experiences of the initial baby boomers. He had several siblings and lived in a rapidly growing community (between 1950 and 1960, Modesto's population more than doubled from 17,400 to 36,600 [Stanley Bare 1999: 111, 116]). He grew up with television, rock 'n' roll and teen movies; he visited the newly opened Disneyland theme park, moved to the suburbs with his parents, had enough money to participate in an increasingly consumerist society and became involved in a distinctive youth culture, most notably through owning a car which he customised and raced (Jones 2016: 9–37; Taylor 2016: 18–32, 49–51). He was also made aware of the horrifying threat of nuclear war through civil defence training films and 'duck and cover' drills at school (Taylor 2016: 19).

Lucas finished high school in 1962 and went on to college (first in his home town before, in 1964, moving on to film school in Los Angeles). After completing his undergraduate studies, he expected to be drafted into the army and perhaps to have to serve in Vietnam, a fate he avoided because he was diagnosed with diabetes in 1966 (Jones 2016: 65; Taylor 2016: 62). Lucas's film projects in the second half of the 1960s indicate his strong interest in current affairs (*Look at Life*, *Apocalypse Now*), his continuing engagement with developments in youth culture (*The Emperor*), and his increasingly critical view of contemporary society, in particular its consumerism and its political leadership (notably that of Richard Nixon who was elected president in 1968), as well as his concern about possible global destruction (the societies depicted in *THX 1138: 4EB* and *THX 1138* are presumably located underground as a consequence of nuclear war or some form of ecological disaster).

Lucas's development from his teenage car obsession to his bleak vision, in *THX 1138*, of where technology, consumerism and politics might take American society reflected an important development across his generation.[13] Like Lucas, the majority of baby boomers (especially, but not exclusively, those who were white and middle-class) grew up in considerable material comfort due to the postwar economic boom, in particular when compared with previous generations.

Their parents had experienced the Great Depression and the austerity of the war years during their childhood and youth. Quite unlike their parents, as young children and teenagers baby boomers were given unprecedented encouragement for self-expression and self-realisation (not least due to the rise of so-called 'permissive' child rearing [Petigny 2009: 37–41]), and they had money to spend which made them a lucrative market for the producers and retailers of consumer goods and services, including popular culture (Cohen 2003: 318–20; Palladino 1996: 97–115). The single most expensive item they purchased was a car. Previously only available to a minority of teenagers, possession of a (often second-hand) car was now becoming a new standard for middle-class and working-class kids alike (cp. Cross 2018: 16–136).

The massive impact their large number had on American society encouraged baby boomers to develop a distinct generational identity, albeit one inflected by diverse and rapidly evolving taste cultures (differentiated along the lines of, for example, ethnicity, race, class and gender). This generational identity was enhanced by spending so much time together in school, with graduation from high school being a shared experience for most young people (over 60% of 17-year-olds graduated from high school in the late 1950s and about 75% by the mid 1960s, as compared to 49% in 1940). Subsequent college attendance became much more common as well; in 1970 about 22% of the population had gone, or were going, to university, as compared to about 10% in 1940 (Wattenberg 1976: 379–80). In addition, baby boomers were the first generation growing up in the knowledge that not only their individual lives but their whole world could be destroyed at any time in a nuclear war (cp. Krämer 2014: 8–9).

One of the consequences of permissive childrearing, material comfort, extensive education, a strong generational identity and an awareness of the nuclear threat was that baby boomers were less inclined than previous generations to accept traditional values and established institutions. When major sociopolitical changes (to do with Civil Rights, second-wave feminism, the student movement, the counterculture, the sexual revolution, anti-Vietnam war protests, environmentalism, etc.) got under way in the 1960s, the first wave of baby boomers born in the 1940s and early 1950s made up an increasing share of supporters of various causes (although leaders tended to be older). The general liberalisation, particularly dramatic in the 1960s and early 1970s, of attitudes and values (as measured by opinion polls) in the United States affected baby boomers, especially the unusually large number of college students among them, more than older people (cp. Krämer 2005: 68–78). As a consequence, a substantial number turned against the kind of lifestyle requiring a conventional career so as to sustain high consumption levels, and experimented with, or at least dreamt about, alternatives. Lucas, for one, did not take over his father's business, as had been expected of him (Jones 2016: 29, 36; Taylor 2016: 56); instead he went to film school and made experimental movies.

Although their experience of the 1960s was darkened by Cold War crises (notably in Berlin in 1961 and Cuba in 1962), assassinations, violent clashes between demonstrators and police, and the Vietnam war, older baby boomers largely maintained an optimistic outlook on the possibility of positive social change (cp. Krämer 2005: 77–8). This outlook was underpinned by ongoing economic growth which ensured the material well-being of most baby boomers and suggested that social problems might eventually be alleviated without too many, or indeed any, sacrifices on the part of the broad American middle class. By the early 1970s, however, baby boomers, like Americans in general, had become aware of extensive environmental damage caused by industrial production, mass traffic and all kinds of waste (Erskine 1972: 120–35), and of likely future shortages of various natural resources needed for continued economic growth, two problems exacerbated by the rapid increase of the global population (Robertson 2012: 61–181). In addition, after decades of economic growth, there was a severe economic downturn, early signs of which could be detected already in the late 1960s (Cohen 2003: 388–9). By the mid 1970s, rising inflation, declining real income and increasing unemployment (an unusual combination of negative developments which came to be known as 'stagflation') pushed the economy to the top of the agenda in polls asking Americans about 'the most important problem facing the country today' (Smith 1980: 168–9).

In light of these developments, which coincided with a series of political calamities (among them the Watergate scandal which led to Nixon's resignation in August 1974, and the non-victorious outcome of the Vietnam war, with the US signing a peace treaty in January 1973 and the US-backed government of South Vietnam surrendering in April 1975), it is not surprising to find that, according to numerous surveys, a sense of decreasing life satisfaction and a more pessimistic outlook on the future of the United States spread across the population (Ladd and Bowman 1998: 28, 31, 44–6; Veroff, Douvan and Kulka 1981: 55–8, 77, 88–9, 528–9, 533–4).

At the same time, the oldest baby boomers born in the 1940s and early 1950s were now old enough to start looking back on their teenage years. This was particularly appealing because these years represented a previous stage in their lives and a time during which people had still

been able unthinkingly to enjoy high levels of consumption and to believe that – as long as nuclear war could be avoided – there would be no
limit to further increases.[14] It is worth noting, though, that in the 1970s
the early baby boomers, especially those with a college education, were
not only the demographic group that worried most about the future,
but also the one most likely to declare childhood and adolescence the
unhappiest periods in their lives (Veroff, Douvan and Kulka 1981: 60,
74, 100). Evocations of the recent past thus responded to baby boomers' longing for a time different from the worrisome present and future, yet involved encounters with in places painful memories as well.

George Lucas and the New Hollywood

Born into a rather conservative family and, as the only boy, destined
to take over his father's business (a stationary store selling everything
from typewriters to toys), George Lucas was an unlikely candidate for
a movie career; for a long time, he did not even show much interest in
cinemagoing (Jones 2016: 9–16, 26; Taylor 2016: 18–21). As a child, Lucas was primarily focused on toys, comics, radio and television (where
he saw many films originally made for theatrical release), and then, as
a teenager, on rock 'n' roll music and cars (Jones 2016: 17–39; Taylor
2016: 20–32, 49–52). Yet, after two years of studying arts, humanities
and social sciences at Modesto Junior College, he left his home town
to attend the University of Southern California (USC) film school in
Los Angeles, his attendance at this expensive private university being
paid for by his father (Jones 2016: 40–5; Taylor 2016: 53–6).

In addition to his longstanding interest in fine art, design and
photography, Lucas's decision for film school was due to the fact that
he had belatedly developed a strong interest in the cinema, especially
in art house and avant-garde movies. He had made some 8mm films
and, through a shared obsession with car racing, befriended the much
older cinematographer and documentary filmmaker Haskell Wexler
(born in 1922), who became a mentor to him.[15] At USC Lucas joined
a group of talented young filmmakers (most of them baby boomers)
who, together with their peers at other film schools, notably those at
the University of California at Los Angeles (UCLA) and New York
University (NYU), were aiming to make inroads into – more or less
mainstream – movie production (Jones 2016: 46–64; Taylor 2016:
56–62; also see Pye and Myles 1979).

After graduation in 1966, Lucas earned some money as a freelance
film editor and cinematographer, before returning to USC at the beginning of 1967 as a postgraduate student and teaching assistant,

continuing to make short documentaries and experimental films (Jones 2016: 64–83; Taylor 2016: 62–7). He expected to continue in this vein, dividing his time between paid work on other people's projects and making his own non-commercial shorts on the side. But then, not long after their first meeting in the late summer of 1967, he was encouraged to develop a feature by Francis Ford Coppola, an older film school graduate (b. 1939) who had already established himself as a Hollywood writer and director (Jones 2016: 84–8; Taylor 2016: 67–9). With Coppola's support, Lucas managed to get funding from Warner Bros. for expanding one of his short films from 1967 into a feature. The production of *THX 1138* was part of a hugely ambitious scheme Coppola and Lucas came up with in 1968/69, whereby they would gather young filmmakers, including Lucas's USC classmate John Milius (b. 1944), in San Francisco so as to enable them to collaborate on a range of feature film projects (Jones 2016: 90–1, 98–111; Taylor 2016: 90–100). This was done under the auspices of a new company called American Zoetrope.

Warner Bros. had been willing to invest in *THX 1138* and other American Zoetrope projects because, throughout the late 1960s and early 1970s, the major Hollywood studios were revising their basic business model of the preceding decades, at the heart of which was the provision of filmic entertainment in principle suitable for all demographic groups, including young children, with an emphasis on female preferences (Krämer 1999: 96). This orientation towards an all-inclusive mass audience was particularly important for Hollywood's most expensive productions, which tended to be its biggest hits. Most of these 'blockbusters' (a term widely used since the 1950s) were musicals, historical epics or international adventures given a special, so-called 'roadshow' release, whereby a film was initially only shown in very few cinemas at high prices, often with all the trappings – such as advance bookings, musical overtures and an intermission – of a night out at the legitimate (musical) theatre (Krämer 2005: 19–29).

Yet in the late 1960s, in the wake of the enormous success of films like *The Sound of Music* (Wise, 1965) and *Doctor Zhivago* (Lean, 1965), Hollywood studios flooded the market with roadshow releases and, as a consequence of this oversupply, most of them flopped, while medium- and even low-budget films, many of them formally and stylistically innovative (Beck 2016; Berliner 2010), were surprisingly successful at the box office as well as with critics (Krämer 2005: 6–19, 40–58; cp. Russell and Whalley 2018: 85–101; Hall and Neale 2010: 184–92). What is more, after the major studios, in 1966, had in effect suspended their previously rigorous self-censorship (through the Production Code, which was eventually replaced with an age ratings system in 1968), they released a large number of high-profile productions that broke long-established filmic taboos to do, among other things, with sex, violence, race and religion (Krämer 2005: 47–58). Examples include some of the highest-grossing films in the United States of the late 1960s, in several cases even of all time, ranging from Warner Bros.' shockingly violent *Bonnie and Clyde* (Penn, 1967), Embassy's erotically charged *The Graduate* (Nichols, 1967) and Columbia's *Guess Who's Coming to Dinner* (Kramer, 1967), a film about interracial marriage, to Paramount's sacrilegious *Rosemary's Baby* (Polanski, 1968), United Artists' homoerotic *Midnight Cowboy* (Schlesinger, 1969) and Columbia's sex-drugs-and-rock 'n' roll road movie *Easy Rider* (Hopper, 1969) (105–10).

Such films were particularly appealing to youth audiences, most especially educated urbanites, while alienating some audience segments, particularly among women (Krämer 2005: 7, 58–62). Because the number of youthful (and educated) cinemagoers was swelled by the growing up of the first wave of baby boomers, Hollywood was increasingly willing to turn its back on older (and less educated) audience members, especially women, as well as on their young children, and instead to focus many of its efforts specifically on teenagers and people in their twenties, with an emphasis on male movie preferences (Krämer 1999: 96–7). The major studios invested heavily in young filmmakers who were assumed to be in touch with the interests and preferences of the youth audience. As it turned out, many of these investments did not pay off (with a particularly large number of flops in 1970 and 1971 [Godfrey 2018; Russell and Whalley 2018: 106–15; Cook 2000: 162–72]). Attendance levels in American cinemas sank to a historic low and several of the major studios made huge losses between 1969 and 1971 (Finler 1988: 286–8).

As already mentioned, Warner Bros., for one, was not at all happy with the initial American Zoetrope production, Lucas's *THX 1138*, and subsequently withdrew funding from all the company's projects in development at the time (some of these were later realised in different contexts, among them Coppola's *The Conversation* [1974] and *Apocalypse Now* [1979]). Coppola and Lucas each followed the demise of the American Zoetrope studio with a huge hit movie: *The Godfather* (1972), a Paramount production, and *American Graffiti*. Other American Zoetrope filmmakers also eventually managed to make it in Hollywood in the 1970s. Indeed, by the beginning of the next decade, these filmmakers, together with their film school peers, chief among them George Lucas's friend Steven Spielberg (b. 1946), had become a transformative force in the American film industry (Russell and Whalley 2018: 143–97).

They had been responsible for a series of huge blockbusters, most of which returned to the previous Hollywood ideal of all-inclusive mass entertainment, or family entertainment if we understand 'family' to refer to young children and their parents as well as teenagers and young adults (Krämer 2005: 89–103). As a consequence, ticket sales increased dramatically and studio profits rose to record levels in the late 1970s (Finler 1988: 286–8). These blockbusters, among them the very highest-grossing films of all time in the United States, included the Spielberg-directed *Jaws* (1975), *Close Encounters of the Third Kind* (1977) and *E.T. The Extra-Terrestrial* (1982); *Grease* (directed by USC film school graduate Randal Kleiser, b. 1946) and *National Lampoon's Animal House* (directed by John Landis, b. 1950); as well as the George Lucas productions *Star Wars*, *The Empire Strikes Back* (Kershner, 1980), *Raiders of the Lost Ark* (Spielberg, 1981) and *Return of the Jedi* (Marquand, 1983) (Krämer 2005: 89–91). Together with Spielberg, Lucas was the leader of this particular pack.

The period in American film history from the mid 1970s onwards, characterised, among other things, by a renewed commitment to family entertainment and so clearly dominated by Lucas, Spielberg and other members of the so-called 'film school generation', is often referred to as the 'New Hollywood', the same term that had previously been used to capture the transformation of Hollywood cinema – *away* from traditional family entertainment – across the 1960s and especially from 1967 onwards (Krämer 1998: 295–305). To avoid confusion, it is advisable, when specifically discussing the formally and thematically innovative films of the late 1960s and early to mid 1970s to use the label 'Hollywood Renaissance' (Krämer and Tzioumakis 2019: xiii–xxvii).

This phrase was inspired by a *Time* story from 8 December 1967, in which the magazine, featuring pictures from *Bonnie and Clyde* on its cover, declared that mainstream American cinema was undergoing a 'renaissance', that is a period of great artistic achievement based on 'new freedom' and widespread experimentation (Kanfer 1967/1971: 333). The cover story was the culmination of a long-running debate about the problematic state of the American film industry. Given that cinema attendance, studio profits and the number of films being made by the majors had declined dramatically between the mid 1940s and the mid 1960s, and half of the eight major studios of the 1930s and 1940s had either closed down or been taken over by 1966 (Krämer 2005: 79; Finler 1988: 280, 286–7), it is not surprising to find that there was much talk about the death of the old Hollywood – and its potential rebirth (Krämer 1998: 294–7).

Most of the filmmakers driving this renaissance, while being unusually young and well-educated by traditional Hollywood standards, were neither baby boomers nor film school graduates. Instead, they were mostly born between the early 1920s and the mid 1930s, receiving their training, and first establishing their reputations, in television or the theatre before breaking into the film industry in the 1960s (Krämer 2005: 82–4). When, in 1967, this group of filmmakers transformed Hollywood cinema with films like *Bonnie and Clyde* (directed by Arthur Penn, b. 1922) and *The Graduate* (Mike Nichols, b. 1931), the film school generation, with few exceptions like Coppola – who had already made the Warner Bros. release *You're a Big Boy Now* (1966) as well as three earlier, independently produced and distributed exploitation movies – was not yet involved in mainstream film production. But that year Lucas completed his most ambitious short film, *THX 1138: 4EB*, which deeply impressed Spielberg, when it was screened at a student film festival, and led to their first meeting. Lucas also went to Warner Bros. on a scholarship and became an assistant on Coppola's Fred Astaire musical *Finian's Rainbow* (1968) (Taylor 2016: 65–8; Jones 2016: 83–9, 92–3). The stage was set for *THX 1138* and *American Graffiti, Star Wars* and *Raiders of the Lost Ark*, although at this point there was not yet any indication that Lucas would one day transform the film industry.

That he eventually did exactly that was only possible due to the support of older teachers and mentors, and his close collaboration with his baby boom contemporaries. On all of his first three features Lucas worked with people he knew well, including Wexler (who was involved in the production of *American Graffiti*) and Coppola (*THX 1138* and *American Graffiti*) as well as Lucas's USC classmates Walter Murch (b. 1943; *THX 1138* and *American Graffiti*) and Willard Huyck (b. 1945; *American Graffiti*), plus the latter's wife Gloria Katz (b. 1942 and a graduate of UCLA film school; *American Graffiti*). Furthermore, one of the editors on Lucas's first three features was his wife Marcia (b. 1945, in Modesto), who he had met on a professional assignment in 1966. Lucas had gotten this assignment through Verna Fields (b. 1918), a well-established Hollywood professional who was teaching at USC film school at the time and later received an editing credit for *American Graffiti* (Jones 2016: 69–71; Taylor 2016: 63). On *Apocalypse Now* Lucas worked closely with Milius and Gary Kurtz (b. 1940), a Vietnam veteran who had graduated from USC film school in 1962 and later (co-)produced *American Graffiti* and *Star Wars*.

George Lucas and *American Graffiti*

In addition to involving many of the same collaborators, George Lucas's films across the second half of the 1960s and the 1970s were characterised by remarkable thematic continuities. These derived, for example, from his interest in Science Fiction, which connects *THX 1138: 4EB*, *THX 1138* and *Star Wars*, and his concern about global catastrophe (already his very first short at film school ended with three provocative title cards: 'Anyone for survival', 'End' and '?', and in *Star Wars* a whole planet explodes). His fascination with cars and/or speed is in evidence in his third and fourth short films – *Herbie* and *1:42:08* (both 1966, the former a study of night-time reflections on a car's shiny surface, the latter a dynamic short about a race car doing laps) (Jones 2016: 60–4; Taylor 2016: 60–1) – as well as in his first three features (among other things, *THX 1138*, *American Graffiti* and *Star Wars* all contain climactic high-speed races).

The theme of escape links his second short film *Freiheit* (1966; a man is shot while trying to cross a border) to *THX 1138: 4EB* (a man escapes from a futuristic underground society) and his first three features (Jones 2016: 57–8, 73–7; Taylor 2016: 60, 64–5). All three tell the story of a young man leaving home to begin a new life elsewhere, the promise of this new beginning being counterbalanced by the certainty of tremendous loss. Another way of putting this is to say that these films deal with (symbolic) death and rebirth.[16] The protagonist of *THX 1138* leaves everything and everyone he has ever known behind and emerges from an underground world into a desert landscape at the end, his liberation being overshadowed by questions about his ability to survive on his own in this new environment. The orphaned protagonist of *Star Wars* has to deal with the death of his foster parents and of his mentor, and in doing so learns that death does not have to be the end (Obi-Wan Kenobi's spirit continues to communicate with him) and is himself reborn as a Jedi warrior with access to the mystical power of 'the Force'. Crucially, unlike the title character of *THX 1138*, Luke finds a secure place in a new community after he leaves home.

American Graffiti does not only tell the story of the one character who leaves town, but also of several others who stay behind. On two occasions, characters question whether it makes sense to leave home so as to find a new home elsewhere. To emphasise how much is at stake in the decision to stay or leave, the main characters' stories are haunted by death. The oldest of them, 22-year-old car mechanic and drag racer John Milner (played by Paul Le Mat, b. 1945),[17] is aware of the dangers of racing, reeling off a litany of fatal accidents when he takes Carol Morrison (Mackenzie Phillips, b. 1959), a 13-year-old girl he gets lumbered with, to a car junkyard. In the film's climactic race, his challenger, 22-year-old Bob Falfa (Harrison Ford, b. 1942) as well as head cheerleader Laurie Henderson, aged 17 (Cindy Williams, b. 1947) – who came along for the ride to spite her boyfriend, former class president Steve Bolander, aged 18 (Ron Howard, b. 1954) – almost die when their car veers off the road, rolls over, catches fire and explodes.

Laurie's 18-year-old brother Curt (Richard Dreyfuss, b. 1947) who, together with Steve, is meant to leave for college on the East Coast the next morning but has grave doubts about this move, has a run-in with a local gang, who jokingly talk about killing people. His ex-girlfriend Wendy (Deby Celiz) reveals that Curt aspires to meet and perhaps work for John F. Kennedy, an ambition forever thwarted, the viewer knows, by the president's assassination the following year. Curt, Steve and John's friend, 17-year-old Terry 'Toad' Fields (Charles Martin Smith, b. 1953) brags about hunting for sport so as to impress Debbie Medway, aged 19 (Candy Clark, b. 1947), a good-time girl he picks up on the street, but he is scared when they walk around the countryside and she will not stop talking about a serial killer active in the area. The captions at the end of the film reveal that in 1973 Steve, who decided to attend the local college, is an insurance agent in Modesto, while Curt, who left for an East Coast university and now is a writer, has moved to Canada, presumably to avoid the draft; Terry went missing in action in Vietnam (which almost certainly means that he is dead),[18] and John died in a car accident.

The film's concluding focus on the death of two of its central characters echoed the prevalence of dying protagonists in many of the key films of the late 1960s and early 1970s, including *Bonnie and Clyde*, *Midnight Cowboy*, *Easy Rider* and *The Godfather*. In addition, there are obvious historical reasons for the prominence of death in this film set in 1962. From the perspective of the early 1970s, when Lucas made *American Graffiti*, it was almost unavoidable to consider how the film's young male characters would be affected by the Vietnam war, in which 2.7 million Americans, most of them baby boomers, served,[19] while a much larger number of young people had, like Lucas himself, lived for years in the shadow of the draft, that is the possibility of being called up to compulsory military service.

In fact, the often-heard claim that the Vietnam war was the defining event for the baby boom generation (as well as for those slightly older) is borne out by a survey conducted in 1985, which asked Americans aged 18 and older about the two most important 'national or world events or changes' of the previous 50 years (Schuman and Scott 1989: 362). For those born between 1941 and 1967, the Vietnam war came out on top (named by around 30% of respondents in this age group, whereas older people tended to judge the Second World War to be most important), and the Kennedy assassination was not far behind in the ranking of key events (with around 10% of baby boomers selecting it; 365–6).

Importantly, the threat of nuclear war was named by around 10% of those born between 1941 and 1967 (Schuman and Scott 1989: 367–8). In the script for *American Graffiti* Lucas had originally intended to mention, through dialogue references, props and radio news items (Lucas, Katz and Huyck 1972: 13, 48, 110; also see the published script, Lucas, Katz and Huyck 1973: 68, 168), the nuclear threat in general and, more specifically, the build-up to the Cuban Missile Crisis, which occurred in October 1962, only a few weeks after the night during which the film is set. In light of the fact that the Cuban Missile Crisis was widely perceived to have brought the United States and the Soviet Union to the brink of nuclear war and thus close to the killing of millions of people (with the survivors perhaps being forced into underground shelters), it is not so surprising that Lucas's retrospective view of the early 1960s was overshadowed by (the prospect of) death.

Last but not least, there were very personal reasons for his foregrounding of death in the story he wanted to tell about his teenage years. In June 1962, shortly before graduating from high school, he had nearly died in a car crash (Jones 2016: 37–9; Taylor 2016: 51–2). Later he would repeatedly identify this as a turning point in his life, insofar as his interests shifted, in the wake of the accident, away from deep immersion in all aspects of car culture to academic study and eventually to filmmaking. According to Lucas, the people pulling him out of his damaged car 'thought I was dead. I wasn't breathing and I had no heartbeat. [...] The accident coincided with my graduation from high school, a natural turning point. Before the accident, I never used to think. Afterward, I realized I had to plan if I was ever to be happy' (quoted in Harmetz 1983/1999: 140).

Among the subjects Lucas studied was anthropology (Jones 2016: 40; Taylor 2016: 53), which must have focused his attention on the importance in cultures all around the world of the transition from one life-stage to another, especially from youth to adulthood – one of the key concerns of both *American Graffiti* and *Star Wars* –, whereby such transitions are often conceptualised in terms of symbolic death and rebirth, paralleling the near-fatal accident and miraculous survival he had experienced himself. Also, as already noted, from the outset Lucas's filmmaking (including the 8mm amateur movies he made at race tracks) repeatedly focused on the beauty and movement of cars, and on the thrilling evocation of rapid motion. One might say that Lucas substituted the cinematic thrills of motion pictures for the real dangers of car racing, most directly in the climactic scene of *American Graffiti*.

By echoing Lucas's own transformative experience, the near-fatal car crash at the end of the film signals a need for radical change, because the old ways can lead to disaster (John dying in a car crash/ Lucas almost getting killed in one), while self-reinvention (Curt leaving Modesto and becoming a writer/Lucas leaving Modesto and becoming a filmmaker) offers hope for a better future. In the interviews he gave to promote the original release of *American Graffiti*, Lucas pointed out that, while the film was meant to recreate the glamour, warmth and fun of teenage life in a bygone era, its message was all about change: 'you know that when the story ends America underwent a drastic change' (Gardner 1973: D40); '[y]ou can't fight change on any level. I guess that's the only statement I was making in the film' (Klemesrud 1973: D13).

And yet, there is a lot of sympathy in *American Graffiti* for the characters who stay in their home town and are likely to carry on with many of their everyday routines but have learnt valuable lessons about themselves and relationships, which could be the foundation for improvements in their lives. In the film, there are two adult characters who offer differing perspectives on what is involved in staying put. The first is one of Curt's former teachers, who went away for college but returned after only one semester, and now appears to be having an affair with one of his pupils, which, apart from anything else, is rather regressive. The second is Wolfman Jack (b. 1938). When Curt goes to the radio station at the edge of town from which Wolfman Jack transmits the show the young people in town are listening to, it becomes obvious that, while the middle-aged disc jockey encourages Curt to explore the 'whole big beautiful world', he himself is quite content to stay, presumably because of the important role he plays in the local community. Of course, George Lucas had moved back to Northern California in 1969, and never left again (Skywalker Ranch would be located close to San Francisco), revolutionising the world of popular entertainment while living less than a two-hour drive from his home town.

Outline

In this book, then, I show that George Lucas made *American Graffiti* at a turning point in his career, when after a decade-long involvement, as a cinemagoer and filmmaker, with alternatives to mainstream Hollywood productions (art cinema, experimental film, documentary, a highly unconventional debut feature), he felt the need to reach a mass audience with his second feature. I argue that the resulting film is best understood as an exploration of (potential) turning points in the lives of its mostly teenaged protagonists, which have to do with the transition from one life-stage to another, and with general changes in

American society as well as with Lucas's own biography and the development of the older members of the baby boom generation.

American Graffiti was meant both to celebrate a certain teenage way of life in the early 1960s and to emphasise the necessity and inevitability of individual and social change, to register both the losses and the opportunities that come with change. This duality, I argue, was at the centre of the film's marketing and of its appeal to an audience mainly made up of baby boomers, who could use the film to reflect on their own teenage past or to see their current teenage lives reflected on screen, and to consider broader historical changes across the preceding decade, among them an increasingly critical attitude, characterising the population as a whole and baby boomers in particular, towards the viability of established institutions and lifestyles.

In emphasising change and critical attitudes in my discussion of the film's story, marketing and reception, I go against much academic writing about *American Graffiti* which, usually taking inspiration from Fredric Jameson's brief comments on this particular movie, and on the 'nostalgia film' in general, in his foundational work on postmodernism (Jameson 1984: 66–8), interprets it as being, first and foremost, an escapist, even reactionary, exercise in nostalgia.[20] In scholarly critiques of *American Graffiti*, 'nostalgia' tends to be used as a negative evaluative term in conjunction with the claim that the film superficially evokes and glorifies a past that never existed, encourages viewers to escape into this imaginary past instead of engaging with the pressing issues of the contemporary world, and, more generally, de-historicises and de-politicises both the present and the past. These critiques of *American Graffiti* are, as I hope to show, at odds not only with the film itself (a detailed analysis of which is the subject of Chapter 2), but also with the intentions of its makers (see Chapter 1) and marketers (Chapter 3), and with how it was understood by contemporary reviewers and resonated in the wider culture (Chapter 3).

Rather than referencing Jameson, my discussion is based on dictionary definitions of 'nostalgia' and scholarly publications about the psychological condition so named. According to the *Oxford English Dictionary*, 'nostalgia' can be understood as a fairly neutral, descriptive term referring to '[a]cute longing for familiar surroundings', 'homesickness', '[s]entimental longing for or regretful memory of a period of the past, esp. one in an individual's own lifetime' or 'sentimental imagining or evocation of a period of the past'.[21] In a sense, the story of *American Graffiti* shows how Steve gets a foretaste (not least through the car crash in which Laurie almost dies) of the longing, homesickness and regret he would feel if he left town as planned, and consequently decides to stay, while Curt initially is so attached to 'familiar surroundings' that he doubts the wisdom of his plan to leave but eventually concludes that it is the right thing to do. Perhaps his decision is helped by the knowledge that the place and the people he leaves behind will always stay with him in his 'sentimental', emotion-filled memories and imagination.

A recent empirical study found that nostalgic feelings occur quite frequently in most people's lives; that they are more likely to arise if people are in a negative mood (especially when they feel lonely); that the primary focus of nostalgia is on important people and momentous events in one's life, in particular with regards to a person's close connections with others; that people's private nostalgic memories often move from recalling problematic situations to remembering their positive resolution; and that, despite the evocation of some negative feelings, such memories make people feel better about themselves and the world at large as well as more socially connected, and therefore presumably better able to act in the present.[22] Nostalgia, then, can be a productive coping strategy in times of crisis.

Notes

1 So as not to clutter the text of this introduction, I provide only minimal references here, mostly to two recent books on George Lucas (Jones 2016; Taylor 2016).

2 For a detailed discussion of Lucas's early film work up to 1971, see Krämer (2022: 35–62).

3 A later novelisation of both *American Graffiti* and its sequel *More American Graffiti* (Norton, 1979) gives the date as 15 September 1962 (Minahan 1979: 18). I am not dealing with *More American Graffiti* in this book but I do think that this fascinating film deserves more attention than it has received so far.

4 See http://www.classictvhits.com/tvratings/1960.htm (also click on subsequent years). All information on ratings charts is taken from this website. All websites referenced in this book were last accessed on 31 October 2021.

5 Information on Wolfman Jack is taken from Jack (1995: 119–219), Huff (2011: 416–7), https://en.wikipedia.org/wiki/Wolfman_Jack and https://www.wolfmanjackradio.com/biography.

6 Information about the film and television careers of particular actors is taken from the Internet Movie Database (https://www.imdb.com/), unless noted otherwise.

7 Figures for the average budget of a Hollywood movie vary, most likely because some refer only to releases by major studios while others take into account films released by smaller distributors. According to Steinberg (1980: 50), the average budget was $1.75 million in 1971 and 'more than' $2.5 million in 1974, while, according to Finler (1988: 36), it was $2.5 million in 1965 and $4 million in 1975. An average budget of around $3 million in 1973 is a reasonable compromise.

8   See https://www.boxofficemojo.com/title/tt0069704/?ref_=bo_se_r_1.

9   According to the inflation-adjusted all-time US chart, as of 31 October 2021, only 20 films released before 1973, and only 25 films released before 1979, have higher earnings then *American Graffiti*; see https://www.boxofficemojo.com/chart/top_lifetime_gross_adjusted/?adjust_gross_to=2019&ref_=bo_cso_ac.

10 Cp. https://en.wikipedia.org/wiki/Mort_Drucker#Mad.

11 The trailer can be found at https://www.youtube.com/watch?v=OZ9G p6Qc8LQ.

12 Most authors use the years 1946 and 1964 to demarcate the baby boom, but others date it differently; generational scholars Neil Howe and William Strauss, for example, use the years 1943 and 1960 (Howe and Strauss 2000: 414). As I show in Chapter 3, in terms of demographic developments 1942 is an appropriate starting point. Nevertheless, in places I use later years according to the sets of statistics available to me.

13 This and the following four paragraphs are informed by Brooks (2009), Steinhorn (2006), Gillon (2004), Douglas (1995), Light (1988), Jones (1980) and Coleman (1961).

14 On fifties nostalgia in the 1970s, see Cross (2015: 92–100), Dwyer (2015), Sprengler (2009: 39–66) and Marcus (2004: 9–35). Also see the extensive literature on *Grease*, most recently Gruner and Krämer (2020). Concurrent with fifties nostalgia, there were the beginnings of a cycle of films about the sixties (Gruner 2016: 1–42).

15 Taylor (2016: 53–5) and Jones (2016: 30–44); on Lucas's 8mm films, see McCarthy (2014: 67–8) and Baxter (1999: 44).

16 This also applies to the Vietnam project Lucas was working on; cp. John Milius's 1969 script for *Apocalypse Now* (Milius 1969).

17 The film does not provide the full names and exact ages of all the characters, but the book published, in the form of a screenplay, in association with it does in most cases (Lucas, Katz and Huyck 1973). Where it does not, it is usually possible to deduce the age from other information. The published screenplay indicates that both Milner and Falfa did not finish high school, having left school at 16 (189).

18 Viewers at the time could not have known or guessed that a few years later Lucas would reveal in *More American Graffiti* that Terry in fact deserted.

19 See https://www.va.gov/OAA/pocketcard/m-vietnam.asp.

20 See Brickman (2014: 44–6, 87–100), Sprengler (2009: 99–102), Langford (2007: 157–76), Shumway (1999: 39–43), Speed (1998: 24–32) and Lewis (1992: 129–37). For revisionist discussions of 'nostalgia' in *American Graffiti* which are more in line with my account see Frances Smith (2018 and 2017: 110–22), Symmons (2016: 159–74, 193–4), Dwyer (2015: 45–76), Godfrey (2014: 118–23) and Dika (2003: 89–94); also see MacKinnon (1984: 134–6) who discusses *American Graffiti* in the context of what he calls 'the American small-town movie'. For early academic discussions of *American Graffiti* in terms of nostalgia, see Le Sueur (1977: 187–97) and Fairchild (1979: 112–9, esp. 117), and the extensive review in *Film Quarterly*, which is probably the first in-depth analysis of the film offering a complex account of its nostalgia (Dempsey 1973: 58–60). Jeff Smith (1998: 172–85) presents an analysis of the film's use of music and Cooper (1974: 283–4) a detailed review of the soundtrack album. For an analysis of Wolfman Jack's role

in *American Graffiti*, in the context of other literary and filmic representations of radio presenters, see Rossi (2009: 85–7), and the cars used in *American Graffiti* are discussed in DeWitt (2010: 47–50). Also see the discussion in Wall and Weber (2020: 15–32) of the historical convergence of cars, radio and music from the 1920s to the early 1960s, which uses youth culture as depicted in *American Graffiti* as a reference point. For a reading of Lucas's first three features as a sustained 'Marcusian Social Critique' of American society, see Decker (2009: 417–41) and Decker (2016: 9–14, 52–73). For a political critique of Lucas's films up to and including *Star Wars* which comes to very different conclusions, see Marez (2016: 119–42). Curtis (1980: 590–601) offers a detailed comparison of *American Graffiti* and *Star Wars*. Intriguingly, one of the first analyses of *American Graffiti* appearing in an academic journal discussed it as a modern epic or myth (Sodowsky, Sodowsky and Witte 1975: 47–55), thus taking an approach similar to the one informing the development, marketing and reception of *Star Wars* as well as much of the scholarly work on that film.

21 See http://www.oed.com/view/Entry/128472?redirectedFrom=nostalgia#eid.
22 See Wildschut, Sedikidis, Routledge and Arndt (2006: 975–93); cp. Bryant, Smart and King (2005: 227–60), which is a study of the role of 'positive reminiscence' in the lives of students in their late teens and early twenties.

1   George Lucas, the New Hollywood and the Making of *American Graffiti*

George Lucas came up with the idea for *American Graffiti* and committed himself to this project for his second feature at a time of profound crisis in his life. This is in evidence in the *San Francisco Chronicle* report containing the first public announcement of Lucas's new project in May 1971, 12 months after Warner Bros. executives had first rejected *THX 1138* at a studio screening and a few weeks after the film's unsuccessful release. The article introduced the filmmaker by declaring that 'he has the temperament of an artist who works alone in an attic' but also has 'a keen business sense aimed at the preservation of his work' (Stone 1971/1999: 3). It described his clashes with Warner Bros. over the final cut and marketing of *THX 1138*, quoting Lucas: 'Sooner or later they decide they know more about making movies than directors. Studio heads. You can't fight them because they've got the money' (6).

American Zoetrope, the company Coppola and Lucas had set up in 1969, was meant to do things differently: 'We say [to filmmakers], "We think you are a talented, functioning person and we are hiring you because of your abilities, and whatever you come up with, we're going to take"' (Stone 1971/1999: 6). Unfortunately, Lucas said, '[p]rimarily because of arguments about *THX*, Warners has cancelled the other six' projects in development at American Zoetrope, and he and Coppola now had 'to figure out a way to make money' (ibid.), Coppola by making the gangster saga *The Godfather*, and Lucas by making what the article described as 'a rock 'n' roll musical comedy of the 50s' (5). By May 1971, then, Lucas was committed to the story that was to become *American Graffiti*, rather than prioritising the Science Fiction and Vietnam projects he had been thinking about (they were not even mentioned in the article).

According to this report, Lucas would adopt a critical perspective on the past. He explained: 'It was a time when the music was inane and everything was like Eisenhower. The most important thing was your

DOI: 10.4324/9781315545509-2

car' (Stone 1971/1999: 5).[1] The author first mentioned Lucas's plan for his second feature immediately after stating that Lucas had received 'a proper Protestant Republican upbringing [in the 1950s], against which he soon rebelled' (ibid.). This echoed an earlier comment declaring that *THX 1138* dealt with 'a chillingly automated society from which one man breaks free. At times, it seemed as if Lucas himself were that man' (3). The comment was meant to refer to Lucas's problematic relationship with Warner Bros., but it also invoked the image of Lucas rebelling against fifties conformity and suggested that his second feature would explore the same 'basically existential' theme as *THX 1138*, summarised by Lucas as follows: 'The importance of self and being able to step out of whatever you're in and move forward rather than being stuck in your little rut' (4).

Lucas insisted that, despite its futuristic setting, *THX 1138* represented the world of today: it was an 'abstraction of 1970' (Stone 1971/1999: 4), which implied that Lucas's second feature might relate to early 1970s America in a similar way. The film was certainly intended to connect with early 1970s Americans who Lucas hoped would turn it into a hit, generating the income needed to keep the dream of making films through American Zoetrope, or its reincarnation in a yet to be formed independent production company, alive.

In the first section of this chapter, I outline developments during the period from Warner Bros.' negative response to the first screening of *THX 1138* in May 1970 to the deal Lucas made with Universal for the production of *American Graffiti* in April 1972. The second section examines the script from May 1972, which Lucas co-wrote with Willard Huyck and Gloria Katz, and which was the basis for the shoot. The third section outlines the completion of the film, its initial rejection by Universal and the resolution of the conflict between Lucas and the studio in the summer of 1973.

May 1970 to April 1972: Initial Idea, Development and Deals

Adhering to the basic principles of American Zoetrope, as a producer Coppola had kept his distance from the making of *THX 1138*, the company's first production, putting his trust in Lucas.[2] Daringly, and perhaps somewhat irresponsibly, Lucas, who was American Zoetrope's vice-president, had created a movie which, unlike the script he had co-written with Walter Murch, made it very difficult to understand the simple story it told, and in places looked and sounded more like one of his experimental shorts than a major studio release.

This was in line with the grand statements that Coppola, as well as many writers impressed by the development deal he had arranged for Lucas with Warner Bros. in 1968 and by the setting up of American Zoetrope in 1969, had been making about the imminent radical transformation of American filmmaking, more radical even than the 'renaissance' announced by *Time* magazine in December 1967. Coppola had declared in 1968: 'I don't think there'll be a Hollywood as we know it when this generation of film students gets out of college' (Lewis 1995: 13; also see 14–5). In this context, making an avant-garde Science Fiction film for studio release may have been an appropriately visionary thing to do – but, professionally, it was a very risky move. It is not altogether surprising that Warner Bros. executives rejected the film when they first saw it in May 1970, insisting on substantial changes. In addition, they threatened to withdraw funding from future American Zoetrope productions and to demand repayment of the money they had loaned the company.

During the next few months, Coppola tried to get six scripts being developed at American Zoetrope into shape so as to convince Warner Bros. of their commercial potential. He also somewhat reluctantly accepted (in September 1970) an offer by Paramount to direct an adaptation of Mario Puzo's 1969 bestseller *The Godfather*. At the same time, in addition to working on *THX 1138*, Lucas had to look for an alternative to *Apocalypse Now*, which had originally been intended as his second feature (John Milius was signed to American Zoetrope in September 1969 and delivered a script in December that year) but was not an attractive commercial proposition. Apart from the idea to do an updated version of classic Science Fiction serials (an excerpt from a 1939 *Buck Rogers* serial opened his original cut of *THX 1138*), which did not appear to have great box office potential either, Lucas considered a semi-autobiographical film about his teenage years in Modesto, partly in response to suggestions by both his wife and Coppola that he should try a more character-based story. Lucas wrote a brief synopsis and then brought Willard Huyck and Gloria Katz on board to write a full treatment.

From the outset, the film was meant to have multiple storylines; later Lucas would say that his original idea had been to make 'a film about four guys who cruise around [...] on the last night of summer' (Sturhahn 1974/1999: 18). Their stories were to be informed by his own experiences:

I spent my teen years cruising the main street in Modesto. [...] I was Terry the toad fumbling with girls. Then I became a drag racer like John. I was interested in cars until a bad accident almost killed me. And I finally became Curt. I got serious and went to college.

(Gardner 1973: D40)

Whereas Huyck and Katz were inclined to emphasise the shortcomings of small-town life, Lucas insisted on a more complex approach. Huyck later said: 'We [Huyck and Katz] put in a lot of stuff about how cruising was this endless cycle of never getting anywhere, and how these people were desperate to get out of town. George said, "This is all great for the treatment, but I loved cruising and I love Modesto"' (Hearn 2005: 46). The film was meant to express this love as well as delivering a critique.

Warner Bros.' negative reaction to the screening of a new cut of *THX 1138* in November 1970 and to the screenplays Coppola submitted at that time threw everything into disarray; the fact that, despite considerable critical acclaim, *THX 1138* eventually earned less than $1 million during its US release in 1971, rounded off the fiasco.[3] Coppola managed to pay back the loan he had received from the studio by reorienting American Zoetrope towards the production of educational and industrial films and renting out equipment, and by making *The Godfather* for Paramount. Lucas, who had attracted considerable media interest as an exceptionally young studio filmmaker, talked about his possible withdrawal from features, arguing that the future of movies lay elsewhere. With regards to American Zoetrope's recent turn to educational and industrial films, he said in the 1971 documentary *George Lucas: Maker of Films* (Hughes): 'There is enough money in it [...] and we're doing something worthwhile. [...] Education is key'. In February 1970, he had told the *San Francisco Examiner* that soon everyone would be making their own movies: 'Think what this will do to our civilization. Movies will replace the pen' (Rubin 2006: 32).

Unlike Coppola, Lucas was not willing to accept studio offers to direct films he had not himself initiated (there was talk about a crime film and two rock movies). He would only get involved in projects he had developed from the outset; it had to be 'something out of your own brain which you then make into a movie' (Sturhahn 1974/1999: 20). His teen comedy fit the bill insofar as it was not only deeply rooted in his biography but also allowed him to rework the teenpics he had seen in his youth and to draw on key elements of his earlier films. Furthermore, the project was in tune with general cultural trends (most notably nostalgia for the 1950s, including a rock 'n' roll revival starting in the late 1960s) and box office hit patterns since 1967

(Krämer 2022: 51–4) to do especially with the success of films featuring rock music on their soundtracks, films about rebellious young people, films set in the fairly recent American past and films about the baby boom generation: the young protagonists of *The Graduate* and *Love Story* (Hiller, 1970), two of the very biggest hits of the years from 1967 to 1970, were all born in the mid 1940s.

Nevertheless, the treatment Lucas had written with Huyck and Katz was rejected by several studios, before he was able to make a deal with United Artists in May 1971, at which time, as discussed above, Lucas started talking about this project to the press. The studio provided $10,000 for developing the treatment into a script (the deal included an option on a second Lucas project, which was to be an as yet untitled Science Fiction/fantasy movie). Because Huyck and Katz were not available, Lucas paid scriptwriter Richard Walter (b. 1944), another recent USC film school graduate, to write the screenplay. When, in the summer of 1971, Lucas read Walter's script, he immediately knew that this was not the story he wanted to film.[4] According to Walter (Dallas 2015), there were two sticking points. First, he had developed the existing treatment to bring it in line with his own coming-of-age in New York, rather than trying to capture Lucas's youth in Modesto – the script was no longer Lucas's own story. Second, Walter had included 'a very sexual scene' that Lucas objected to, not necessarily because he was prudish, as Walter surmised (after all there had been nudity and sex in *THX 1138*), but more probably because Lucas did not want to risk alienating, or through a restrictive rating to discourage or exclude, certain prospective audience segments, especially younger teenagers and women.[5]

Since Lucas had spent the development money from United Artists on Walter, he now had to write the script himself, without getting any money for his efforts, a situation familiar from the time he had worked on *THX 1138*. He later said: '*THX* had taken three years to make and I hadn't made any money. Marcia was still supporting us' with her income from editing jobs; and during the early stages of developing *American Graffiti*, 'I asked Marcia to support us some more' (Vallely 1980/1999: 90–1). At some point during 1971, Lucas decided to set up his own company Lucasfilm Ltd., rather than organising the production of *American Graffiti* through American Zoetrope. Throughout 1971 United Artists' interest in the development deal with Lucas must have been quite strong. In August, the company officially registered the title *The Star Wars* for Lucas's Science Fiction/fantasy project which was included in that deal (Taylor 2016: 106; Rinzler 2007: 6). And on 28 December, Lucas signed another agreement with the distributor concerning his work on *American Graffiti* and his plans for *The Star Wars* (Rinzler 2007: 6). But when he finally submitted his script early in 1972, United Artists did not like it and withdrew from both projects.

Lucas continued revising the script for *American Graffiti*, offering it to various studios until Universal finally showed interest. Despite the fact that this was going to be a low-budget picture, Universal had very little confidence that the film would make enough money at the box office to repay the company's investment. Only when Coppola – now, in the wake of the release of *The Godfather* in March that year, a big name in Hollywood – signed on as the producer of *American Graffiti* on 6 April 1972 was Universal willing to make a deal with Lucas for this film and for two additional projects, presumably *The Star Wars* and *Apocalypse Now* (Rinzler 2007: 6).[6]

The budget for *American Graffiti* was set at $775,000, roughly the same as for *THX 1138*, although average Hollywood budgets had been rising in the meantime and a fair amount of money would be needed for music rights (the soundtrack was meant to feature numerous hits from the 1950s and early 1960s).[7] To keep the budget within this tight limit, Lucas was offered a relatively small upfront salary and a large profit participation deal.[8] Universal was evidently so unsure about the financial viability of Lucas's second film that the studio would only get involved at rock-bottom prices. In fact, Ned Tanen (b. 1931), Universal's head of production since 1970, had more reasons than most executives to stay clear of so-called 'youth-cult' films and (relatively) young filmmakers, having green-lit *Two-Lane Blacktop* (directed by Monte Hellman, b. 1932) and *The Last Movie* (Dennis Hopper, b. 1936), two massive box office flops in 1971 (Cook 2000: 312; cp. Godfrey 2018: 203). So when Tanen decided to finance *American Graffiti*, he remained very cautious. There may also have been specific concerns about Lucas's script for *American Graffiti*, with regards to its unusual title, its complicated multi-strand narrative and what appear to have been rather lifeless characterisations and dialogue (Pollock 1990: 105; Warren and Levine 1975: 52; Sturhahn 1974/1999: 18).

May 1972: The Final Script

With the money provided by Universal, Lucas was able to hire Huyck and Katz, who were now available, for script revisions, mainly to do with fleshing out the characters and improving the dialogue. The only version of the script that I have been able to see is a 'SECOND DRAFT' attributed to Lucas, Katz and Huyck and dated 10 May 1972 (Lucas, Katz and Huyck 1972).[9] Structurally, this script – which has 114 pages and 79 scenes with constant switching between, and the occasional, temporary merging of, four storylines (focusing on Steve and Laurie; Terry, with an important part played by Debbie in this storyline; John, with an important part for Carol; as well as Curt and a cross-section of the town's population, including a mystery woman) – was, according to Lucas, quite close to his initial synopsis and the treatment he had written with Huyck and Katz in 1970.

Yet its tone and attitude differed from the impression he had given the journalist interviewing him in May 1971 for the article in the *San Francisco Chronicle* discussed at the beginning of this chapter. In May 1971, it had seemed that *American Graffiti* would, like *THX 1138* – but now in a brightly comical rather than a darkly serious fashion –, overtly critique American society and culture, including the 'inane' music of the time, and that it would deal, through the figure of a rebellious teenager, with the same 'basically existential' theme as his first feature, to do with freeing oneself from oppressive circumstances (Stone 1971/1999: 4–5). Lucas, Katz and Huyck's second draft script from May 1972 does not – at least not on its surface – present a particularly critical view of small-town life in early 1960s America, and the one character who leaves town in the end (Curt) is far from being a rebel who struggles to break free; instead, he wants to renege on an agreement with his friend Steve about going away to college in the East together. Echoing a scene in *THX 1138*, which shows a prison with no walls, making it possible for THX simply to walk out while other inmates are too scared to do so, Steve admonishes Curt: 'now you want to crawl back into your cell' (Lucas, Katz and Huyck 1972: 4). Steve is the only one who has something bad to say about the place where they live (calling it a 'turkey town' [4]), and he equates the refusal to leave with a reluctance to grow up, holding up their older friend John as a negative example: 'You wanta [sic] end up like John? You can't stay seventeen forever' (5). But in the end, *Steve* decides to stay, not because he is afraid and prefers the safety of a 'cell', but because he values his relationship with Curt's sister Laurie more than what he might find in the East.

At the same time, the script makes it clear that John is not simply 'stuck' in a 'rut', but is fully aware of the dangers associated with his racing and of the fact that he cannot beat all challengers for much longer, and nevertheless chooses to continue. When, towards the end of the story, Terry insists that '[y]ou'll always be number 1', 'John looks at Terry who looks so earnest he has to smile' and agrees – for Terry's sake (110). In fact, John had previously shown his commitment to his friendship with Terry by rescuing him from two 'punks' who were beating him up (99). Finally, there is no indication that the numerous songs listed in the script as accompaniment of individual scenes are meant to be made fun of (for being 'inane'); instead they are clearly intended to comment on the unfolding action and/or to help create a certain atmosphere. In fact, on its very first page, the script declares that in those days 'the music was better'.

The *American Graffiti* script does not – at least not straightforwardly – launch another attack on contemporary America, this time from the perspective of the past rather than, as in *THX 1138*, from the perspective of the future. And yet there are many connections between the *American Graffiti* script and *THX 1138* as well as Lucas's short films; in fact, Lucas reused and reworked elements of almost all of his earlier films. As mentioned above, perhaps the most striking of these have to do with Lucas's fascination with the possibility of comprehensive destruction, in evidence in *Look at Life* and both versions of *THX 1138*.

Lucas, Katz and Huyck's second draft script for *American Graffiti* includes an early scene with John sitting on his car in 'the parking lot of the ACME FALLOUT SHELTER CO', the radio news reporting that 'Russia steps up arms aid to Cuba' (Lucas, Katz and Huyck 1972: 13). This foreshadows the Cuban Missile Crisis in October 1962 and the fate that the United States only narrowly avoided, a fate which would have required millions of desperate people to seek what little protection they could get in fallout shelters. In a later scene, Terry tells Debbie about his intention to join the Marines; she likes the idea on one level – after all '[t]hey got the best uniforms', 'but what if there is a war?'. Terry replies nonchalantly: 'With the bomb, who's going to start it? We'd all blow up together' (48). The future would seem to hold only two alternatives: a fragile peace (sustained by the nuclear strategy of mutual assured destruction) or total devastation.

As far as this script is concerned, then, *American Graffiti* tells, like *Look at Life*, a kind of pre-apocalyptic story as much as the two versions of *THX 1138* tell post-apocalyptic stories. The script links the prospect of nuclear war to the film's action. When the car of John's challenger crashes in the climactic race, it is 'exploding like a small A-bomb blowing it to smithereens and into Modesto history' (Lucas, Katz and Huyck 1972: 110). Debbie's question about the possibility of war quoted earlier most immediately raises the spectre of the Vietnam war, in which Terry will indeed die, according to the 'POSTSCRIPT': 'TERRY FIELDS WAS KILLED BY A VIET-CONG BOOBIE TRAP IN DECEMBER 1964' (114). In the course of the war, American generals and politicians discussed the possible use of nuclear weapons (Tannenwald 2007: 190–240).

Furthermore, the radio news broadcast featuring the item on Cuba mentioned above includes references to 'a Kennedy speech' (thus, together with other references in the script, subtly evoking the president's assassination the following year) and 'the big news, a local psycho killer [who] struck again [...] leaving his trademark, a dead goat's head near the victim' (Lucas, Katz and Huyck 1972: 13), this killer later on becoming the subject of a discussion between Debbie and Terry. In a sense, the deadliness of a possible nuclear apocalypse (together with other biographical and contextual factors discussed in the Introduction) is radiating out across the world of 1962 Modesto in this script, so that the members of the Pharaohs gang talk about killing people, John contemplates the deadly fate of drag racers, and the postscript has two of the four main male protagonists (Terry and John) die. Indeed, references to war, killing and death are everywhere in the *American Graffiti* script (10, 22, 30, 35, 64, 74, 91, 99).

In this respect, the script echoes *THX 1138*. The female protagonist LUH is executed, this kind of punishment apparently being quite common; the whole underground society is permeated by death with frequent work accidents killing hundreds of people; and it is highly doubtful whether THX will be able to survive on the surface. What is more, close to the film's ending, a so-called 'hologram' (actually a television actor), who is trying to escape with THX, crashes his car into a pillar and dies, while THX, pursued by robotic motorcycle cops who also crash, wins the final race to freedom. This establishes another close link between the two features. In the script for *American Graffiti*, John drives safely in the climactic race whereas Bob Falfa crashes, almost killing himself and Laurie.[10]

More generally, the *American Graffiti* script foregrounds the make and look of cars. Even before the first of the young protagonists is introduced, the script describes the arrival of 'a beautiful decked and channeled, candy-apple red, tuck and rolled '53 Merc' (Lucas, Katz and Huyck 1972: 1). Similarly close attention is paid to all the other cars featured in the story. The script is thus closely connected to the rather fetishistic display of car surfaces in *Herbie*, the multiple views, from both close by and far away, of the race car in *1:42.08* and the presence of flashy cars in the underground society of *THX 1138*. There is something excessive about the latter, as there is in the parodic advertisement for a Camaro sports car (represented as a rhinoceros) in *The Emperor*. Rather than simply indulging his car obsession as he had done in *Herbie* and *1:42.08*, Lucas is exposing and questioning it in these later films.

The same applies to *American Graffiti*. When Steve tells Terry, who normally gets around on a 'scooter', that he can have Steve's flashy car while he is away, much is made of Terry's over-the-top emotional response: he is 'frozen to a spot', 'looks hypnotized', cannot speak, moves 'like a robot', has 'a tear rolling down [his] cheek' and finally manages to say: 'I'll – love and protect this car until death do us part' (Lucas, Katz and Huyck 1972: 10–11). Soon afterwards, John laments: 'the strip's shrinking. I can remember about five years back it took two hours and a whole tank of gas to make one circle' (14). For John, sitting in his souped-up car in what is in effect a massive traffic jam, having to move extremely slowly and burning up large amounts of fuel, is a paradisiacal state compared to which the present – with less of a jam and hence less fuel consumption – amounts to a fall from grace.[11] John's and Terry's investment in cars is revealed to be as absurd as the race cars in the underground city of *THX 1138* and the Camaro ad in *The Emperor*. What is more, Curt is first shown in 'a grey, insect-like Citroen duex [sic] chevaux'; it is a 'little car' and it 'putters' (3). Obviously, he is not invested in cars at all, which may have something to do with the fact that he is the only character who actually leaves town.

But this is not to say that, by the end of the script, the other male characters are just as fixated on cars as they appear to be at its beginning. Initially, Steve wants Terry to 'take care of my car' (Lucas, Katz and Huyck 1972: 10) because he seems to think that he cannot trust anyone else to treat the vehicle with the appropriate respect, but he later takes it back because he has to find Laurie, who is about to join in the climactic race as a passenger in Bob Falfa's car. The car has become a means to a romantic end. For Terry, Steve's car is, from the outset, both a valued object in its own right and something to impress girls with, pretending that it is his property. When the truth comes out at the end, Debbie does not mind very much; in response to his revelation that he only has 'a little Vespa', she says: 'Why that's almost a motorcycle. I love motorcycles' (106). At the end of his time with Carol, John allows her to take his car's 'gear shift knob' as something, in her words, 'to remember you by' (Lucas, Katz and Huyck 1972: 91). And, as already mentioned, John only agrees with Terry's claim that he has 'the fastest car in the valley' so as not to disillusion him; John's pretence about his continued racing prowess is an act of friendship. The *American Graffiti* script shows that ultimately cars are in the service of social connections in this small town. Ironically, Curt, who surveys a cross-section of the town's population during the night, does so without his car (he only uses it to drive to Mel's Drive-In at the beginning of the story and to Wolfman Jack's radio station at the edge of town towards its end). And he then leaves everyone behind by flying East in an airplane.

In addition to drawing on Lucas's earlier films, the script is full of autobiographical references, mapping key aspects of his teenage experiences and development onto the main male characters (including Steve, despite Lucas's protestations to the contrary). At the end of the story, Curt leaves town (in 1962) like Lucas did in 1964; and, as the postscript reveals, he eventually becomes 'A WRITER' (Lucas, Katz and Huyck 1972: 114), while Lucas turned into a filmmaker (co-)writing his screenplays.[12] In a conversation with a former teacher of his, Curt reveals that he is going to study anthropology in the East (26). Lucas studied anthropology at the local college from 1962 to 1964, having stayed in town after his high-school graduation just like Steve. From the time he got his driver's license in 1960 until his accident in 1962, Lucas was heavily involved in street racing, just like John. A Freudian slip in the screenplay reveals Lucas's close identification with John. The postscript states that 'JOHN MILNER WAS KILLED BY A DRUNK DRIVER IN JUNE 1962' (Lucas, Katz and Huyck 1972: 114); this is a mistake since the story is supposed to take place at the *end* of the summer of 1962, whereas June 1962 is the month in which Lucas had his near-fatal car accident. Before getting a car, Lucas owned a motorcycle, a bit like Terry whose Vespa is 'almost a motorcycle'. Going even further back into his childhood, we can note that in the script John tricks Carol into revealing where she lives, so that he can take her home; her address is '631 ROMONA' (59), whereas Lucas resided at 230 Ramona Street until he was 12 (in the film Carol's address is 231 Ramona Street).[13]

Thus, the *American Graffiti* script references both Lucas's biography and his earlier films. It also draws on the teen-oriented films Lucas and his co-writers would have seen in their youth, and more generally on the teen culture of the 1950s and early 1960s which they had lived through.[14] Fifties and sixties teen film stars Tuesday Weld, Sandra Dee and Connie Stevens (who was a pop singer, too) are mentioned in dialogue (Lucas, Katz and Huyck 1972: 36, 48). And the script's focus on cars, racing and accidents echoes fifties teen culture. Fetishised vehicles, both motor cycles and cars, as well as the racing and the sometimes lethal accidents associated with them had played an important role in films like *The Wild One* (Kramer, 1953) and *Rebel Without a Cause* (Ray, 1955) and in the publicity surrounding James Dean and his death (the script featuring a dialogue reference to Dean on page 35). Vehicular death was also featured in pop songs (such as 'Teen Angel' [1959], which appears in *American Graffiti*, 'Tell Laura I Love Her' [1960] and 'Leader of the Pack' [1964]). In addition, three important early rock 'n' roll performers (Buddy Holly, Richie Valens and J.P. 'Big Bopper' Richardson) had been killed in a plane crash in 1959 (this incident being referenced on page 30), and Eddie Cochran in a car accident in 1960.

Furthermore, by giving a prominent role to the Pharaohs, the script draws on the youth gangs appearing in 1950s songs (e.g. 'Leader of the Pack') as well as many movies, including the ones mentioned above. Together with other elements of the script (on page 32, for example, Carol says to John: 'You're a regular J.D.', that is juvenile delinquent), the Pharaohs subplot playfully engages with the theme of juvenile delinquency so central to many films for and/or about teenagers, most notably *Blackboard Jungle* (Brooks), a 1955 social problem movie about a teacher and his rebellious and delinquent teenage pupils.

This film is a key reference point for the script because on the very first page it identifies the song playing during the pre-credit and credit sequence as 'Rock Around the Clock'. Initially released on record without much success in 1954, this song by Bill Haley and His Comets was used in the opening credit sequence of *Blackboard Jungle* and thereafter became the first rock 'n' roll single topping the pop charts in the USA and indeed one of the bestselling singles of all time (Dawson 2005). 'Rock Around the Clock' also provided the title for the first-ever rock 'n' roll movie, which told a story about the discovery and breakthrough of an exciting new band played by Bill Haley and His Comets.

Rock Around the Clock (Sears, 1956) marked the screen debut of legendary radio disc jockey Alan Freed, who played a key role in the popularisation of rock 'n' roll, and appeared in several further rock 'n' roll movies as a more or less fictionalised version of his real (professional) self (James 2017: 33–54). This in turn could be seen (together with Lucas's earlier film *The Emperor* and his fascination with DJs during his teen years [Farber 1974/1999: 39]) as the main inspiration for the script's foregrounding of Wolfman Jack, who is the first character mentioned. He is the focus of the pre-credit sequence which begins with the search for a station on a car radio, this search ending when 'a wolf howl shatters through time as the legendary Wolfman Jack hits the airwaves', his patter preceding 'Rock Around the Clock' (Lucas, Katz and Huyck 1972: 1). In addition to being a voice on the radio, later on (99–103) Wolfman Jack appears in the flesh, interacting with Curt and in doing so playing a version of himself much like Alan Freed had done.

Apart from summing up Lucas's early films and his teen years (as well as much of the teen culture of the 1950s and early 1960s), the making of *American Graffiti*, as indicated earlier, brought together many of his previous collaborators as well as his mentors from the preceding decade. Seven of the film's main credits would go to Coppola (producer), Kurtz (co-producer), Lucas (director), Lucas, Katz and Huyck (writers), Wexler ('Visual Consultant [Supervising Cameraman]'), Fields and Marcia Lucas (editors), and Murch ('Sound Montage & Re-recording'). In making a film about the summer after his high-school graduation in 1962 and the years leading up to it (with, as we have seen, Terry, John, Steve and Curt representing different periods in his teen life), Lucas brought together people from various stages in his development from 1962 onwards.

In some ways, the *American Graffiti* script, with its focus on two young couples (Steve and Laurie, Terry and Debbie) and two older mentor figures (Milner, Wolfman Jack) echoed the friendship networks, marriages (George and Marcia Lucas, Huyck and Katz) and the mentoring relationships (with both Wexler and Coppola guiding Lucas) that underpinned the production of the film. One might go as far as saying that in making *American Graffiti* Lucas mainly drew on friends he had made after (like Curt) he had left Modesto, echoing a line in the script which is first spoken by Laurie who is quoting her brother (with Steve saying the same thing later on): 'it doesn't make sense [...] to say goodbye to friends you love just to find new friends' (Lucas, Katz and Huyck 1972: 112, 139). It *does* make sense if these new friends enable one to do new things, like making movies. At the same time, as the research on nostalgia discussed in the Introduction suggests, it is important to remember friendship networks of the past as Lucas did in the story of *American Graffiti*, not least to reaffirm social connections in the present, like the ones he mobilised in the making of the film.

June 1972 to the Summer of 1973: Production, Rejection and Resolution

Throughout the production of *American Graffiti*, Lucas worked closely with Kurtz, while Coppola once again stood back.[15] Casting, location scouting and other pre-production work must have started soon after the Universal contract was signed in April, because, as noted above, the second draft screenplay from 10 May already identified the DJ appearing in the film as Wolfman Jack, and shooting started on 26 June 1972, first in San Rafael, then in Petaluma and other locations in the vicinity of San Francisco. Principal photography ended on 4 August 1972. Given the complexity of the film's intertwining of four storylines and of its soundtrack, which wove Wolfman Jack's patter and the songs he played together with dialogue as well as the sound of cars and other noises,[16] post-production was completed in a surprisingly short period of time. In January 1973 *American Graffiti* was ready for the first screening for studio executives.

To everyone's surprise, Ned Tanen reacted to the film just as negatively as Warner Bros. executives had responded three years earlier to *THX 1138*. This time no-one could accuse Lucas of departing too much from the script the studio had had access to (only relatively minor changes were made between the second draft script and the final film, mainly to do with shortening and streamlining the story as well as removing references to nuclear war and reducing the emphasis on sex), nor that he had made a wilfully opaque film. In fact, overall the audience at that first screening in San Francisco on 28 January 1973 responded enthusiastically to *American Graffiti*. Nevertheless, another battle about re-editing ensued. Lucas must have felt that the, for him, fairly traumatic experience of *THX 1138* was repeating itself.

This was especially shocking because this time he had set out to make a commercial movie and could expect that the studio would recognise its box office appeal. Indeed, by the time of *American Graffiti*'s January 1973 screening, the most recent box office trends confirmed its huge commercial potential. Coppola was now associated with the highest-grossing film of all time in the USA (*The Godfather*, with rentals of $81.5 million by the end of 1972), while two films about the first cohort of baby boomers – *Love Story* ($50 million) and *The Graduate* ($48.3 million) – came fourth and fifth in *Variety*'s all-time chart ('All-Time Box Office Champs' 1973: 30). In October 1972, *Love Story* had become the highest-rated movie ever shown on American television (watched in 42% of all households), while *The Graduate* had had a successful theatrical re-release that year ('Big Rental Films of 1972' 1973: 7).

In 1971/72, coming-of-age stories involving teenagers or those a little bit older had been big business. *Variety*'s end-of-year chart for 1971 listed the romantic drama *Summer of '42* (Mulligan) at number 3 (with rentals of $14 million) and *Love Story* (released in December 1970) at number 1 ('Big Rental Films of 1971' 1972: 9). In addition, there were two films featuring teenagers which were released late in 1971 and made a big impact the following year: the futuristic crime-and-punishment movie *A Clockwork Orange* (Kubrick) ended up in seventh place (with rentals of $12 million) and the 1950s set coming-of-age drama *The Last Picture Show* (Bogdanovich, $12.8 million) in sixth place in the end-of-year chart for 1972; and *Summer of '42* was reissued that year, earning another $4.5 million ('Big Rental Films of 1972' 1973: 7). What is more, the highest grossing Hollywood teen movie of all time, the musical *West Side Story* (Wise, 1961), achieved ratings of 28.9 and 27.1 when it was broadcast in two parts in March 1972 (which means that it was seen in more than a quarter of all American households), and *Gidget Gets Married* (Swackhamer), a made-for-TV sequel to a series of Gidget teen movies of the late 1950s and early 1960s, achieved a 28.5 rating in January 1972 (Steinberg 1980: 34).

Films about teenagers, and those just a little bit older, were certainly in demand in 1971/72, as were films set in the fairly recent past, including *Summer of '42, The Last Picture Show* and *The Godfather*. Indeed, in November 1971, *Variety* had declared: 'this far in 1971, nostalgia seems to be of more proven power [at the box office] than anything else' (Verrill 1971, quoted in Godfrey 2018: 211).[17] The fact that, despite all these good omens, Tanen rejected *American Graffiti* suggests that Lucas's reputation as an uncommercial filmmaker lingered on, overshadowing his genuine attempt to make a hit movie and that there was much about the film itself (foremost perhaps its multiple storylines and odd title as well as the absence of movie stars) which went against the film industry's general expectations for a financially viable theatrical release. Of course, industry expectations had often proved wrong in recent years and, in any case, Tanen had known about the film's special characteristics before agreeing to finance it. It is possible that he had expected a more substantial reworking of the script in the time between Universal making a deal with Lucas in April 1972 and the start of principal photography in June.

Whatever the reasons for Tanen's negative response to the first screening of *American Graffiti* in San Francisco on 28 January 1973 were, Universal initially favoured substantial re-editing, and considered not to give the film a theatrical release at all and show it on television instead, or to give it a brief, wide theatrical release in the summer.[18] The assumption was that, in the case of a negative audience response, a wide release facilitated substantial returns before word got around. Lucas and his collaborators fought hard to keep changes to the film to a minimum and to convince Universal that a narrow theatrical release would make it possible to target the audience segments that were most likely to respond positively to the film and would then start spreading positive word of mouth which could draw in ever more people. Already at the first screening, Coppola made a dramatic gesture by offering to buy *American Graffiti* from Universal and then find another studio to release it (this gesture having some credibility as Coppola had made a lot of money from *The Godfather*). This probably helped to make the case that changes to the version screened in January should be kept to a minimum; in the end only a few minutes were cut.[19]

The shortened version was shown at the Writers' Guild Theater in Beverly Hills on 15 May 1973, and it was received even more enthusiastically by the audience (if not by studio executives) than the version shown in January (Baxter 1999: 147–8; Pollock 1990: 122). This was followed by further highly successful screenings on the Warner Bros. lot and elsewhere in Los Angeles, including Lucas's alma mater, the University of Southern California (Stempel 2001: 109; Baxter 1999: 148; Pye and Myles 1979: 129). The huge success of the *American Graffiti* previews derived, at least partly, from the exceptional efforts of Wolfman Jack to use his radio show to attract people who would respond particularly well to a movie featuring classic rock 'n' roll music (Jack 1995: 228). By 1973, Wolfman Jack was a celebrity who, in addition to his radio programme being broadcast by many stations, toured the country with a live show, brought out 'oldies' albums and from February 1973 onwards regularly appeared on NBC's weekly rock music television show *The Midnight Special* (1972–81) (Jack 1995: 170–219).

Many people in the preview audiences would have been aware of Lucas's personal reputation; his well-received debut feature and the documentary about him were both shown on television in spring 1973 (Taylor 2016: 101; Rinzler 2007: 3; Smith 2003: 26–7; Baxter 1999: 113–4, 146; Pollock 1990: 96–7). With regards to the USC screening in front of people who must have known that Lucas had graduated from the university's film school, Aubrey Solomon reported that he had

> never seen an audience go wild for a movie like at this screening. They were hooting, hollering, and cheering all the way through. I later viewed the movie at a theatre in Montreal where the response was enthusiastic but nothing like the USC screening.
>
> (Stempel 2001: 109)

By June, major critics such as *Newsday*'s Joseph Gelmis had seen, and liked, the film (Baxter 1999: 146–7), and other studios learned that Universal had a potential hit on its hands but seemed unsure what to do with it; indeed, Fox and Paramount offered to take over the film's release (Baxter 1999: 148; Pollock 1990: 122). By the time A.D. Murphy's glowing review of the film – the summary statement read: 'Outstanding evocation of 50s teenagers, told with humor and heart. Strong outlook' (Murphy 1973: 20) – appeared in *Variety* on 20 June, Universal most probably had already decided to roll out the film slowly from August onwards.

Conclusion

Only in his mid twenties, George Lucas had to face a great professional challenge in the early 1970s. Since his first meeting with Francis Ford Coppola in 1967, Lucas's career plans had undergone a most dramatic shift (as discussed in the Introduction). Where previously he had seen his professional future in terms of freelance work as an editor and cinematographer, such paid employment being complemented by the kind of experimental filmmaking he had excelled with at film school, Coppola encouraged and facilitated his transition to making theatrical features, funded and released by the major studios. In addition, Coppola enticed Lucas to join him in setting up and running American Zoetrope, a company around which a community of young filmmakers quickly formed, extending the relative freedom and intense collaboration Lucas and his peers had experienced at film school into the world of features. What is more, on his first feature project Lucas endeavoured to combine his interest in the avant-garde with the production of a genre picture. Another difficult project, the Vietnam movie *Apocalypse Now*, was already designated for his second feature.

But Warner Bros.' negative response to *THX 1138* in May and November 1970, followed by the film's disastrous box office performance in 1971, cast everything – American Zoetrope and its filmmaking community, the various films in the pipeline, even Lucas's prospect of having any kind of viable career in Hollywood – in doubt. At this point, Lucas considered leaving Hollywood behind altogether; and he certainly refused to become a director for hire, filming other people's stories. Instead, by May 1971, he was committed to making a teen comedy that, judging by box office charts and broader cultural trends at the time, appeared to have a good chance of becoming a hit and, due to this prospect, to receive production funding from a major studio, which, after several rejections, was finally achieved when Universal came on board in April 1972. Importantly, the film's story returned Lucas to the time of a previous crisis, his near-fatal car accident in the summer of 1962, a crisis he had not only mastered but turned to his advantage by committing himself to his studies (at Modesto Junior College) which in turn eventually allowed him to develop his long-standing interest in creative endeavours (initially art, design and photography, the latter eventually evolving into a fascination with moving pictures).

The development and production of *American Graffiti* can be seen as an extremely productive use of nostalgia by Lucas, who revisited a past crisis in his life and its resolution, and surrounded himself with mentors and collaborators from the preceding decade, making the very process of deciding on the future direction of one's life the subject of the film that, if all went well, would help him to resolve his current professional problems and secure his future as a Hollywood film-maker. But Lucas's reputation as a maverick as well as certain aspects of *American Graffiti* (notably its title, narrative complexity and lack of stars) apparently troubled Universal so much that the film, even in the shortened version that the studio insisted on, came close to not receiving a proper theatrical release at all.

I now want to take a closer look at *American Graffiti*, examining the film's overall structure and its sequential unfolding. My analysis is based on the version Lucas restored for the film's 1978 re-release (rather than the original release version, which does not appear to be available). The poster for this re-release announced not only that the film was shown '[f]or the first time in full Dolby Stereophonic Sound', but also that it featured 'additional original scenes never shown before'.[20] According to Jim Smith (2003: 38), however, Lucas had already 'reinserted the deleted sequences' into release prints before 1978.

Notes

1 It is unclear whether Lucas initially wanted the story to take place in the late 1950s and only later shifted it to 1962, or whether he had 1962 in mind from the outset, referencing the Eisenhower era (which officially ended when Kennedy took over the presidency in 1961) and 'the 50s' in a way that subsumed the early 1960s. I am inclined to think that it was the latter.

2 This and the following three paragraphs are largely based on Krämer (2022: 35–62).

3 This and the following two paragraphs are once again based on Krämer (2022: 35–62).

4 This paragraph and the next four are largely based on Jones (2016: 135–41), Taylor (2016: 109–10), Kaminski (2008: 35–7), Rinzler (2007: 6–7), Rubin (2006: 47–8), Hearn (2005: 53–5), Smith (2003: 30–3), Schumacher (2000: 130), Baxter (1999: 116–23) and Pollock (1990: 105–8). Also see Warren and Levine (1975: 50–2) and Howard (1973).

5 This is confirmed by the report that Lucas was later unable to make a deal with American International Pictures because there was not enough sex and violence in the film (Baxter 1999: 120–3).

6 Coppola's involvement did not turn *American Graffiti* into an American Zoetrope production; instead Coppola here operated through the Coppola Company.

7 The budget figure varies from source to source. I have taken the one given in Rinzler (2007: 6) and Hearn (2005: 54), because they both had access to original documents from the Lucasfilm corporate archive.

8 Different sources provide different details about Lucas's payment. Several mention an upfront salary of $50,000 for writing and directing, and 20%

of net profits, whereby it is not clear exactly how the latter was to be calculated (Jones 2016: 140, 494; Baxter 1999: 122; Dick 1997: 179). In any case, Lucas's profit participation would eventually make him very rich.

9 There is also a published script (Lucas, Katz and Huyck 1973). Unlike the May 1972 screenplay, it correctly identifies most of the songs being played in the film, and it is much closer to its action and dialogue. However, there are some differences between book and film, which leads me to conclude that the book was probably based on a revised script produced shortly before, or during, principal photography, or perhaps on an early cut of the film.

10 According to Huyck and Katz, in Lucas's earlier version(s) of the script, Laurie actually dies in the climactic car crash (Warren and Levine 1975: 52).

11 The burning of fuel for the sake of burning it (rather than for the sake of getting somewhere) is reminiscent of the plastic cubes purchased by the denizens of the underground city in *THX 1138*; upon arriving home with these cubes, they place them in their 'consumer', which appears to dissolve them – for no recognisable purpose whatsoever other than the act of consumption itself.

12 Curt has a sister; Lucas had three, one of whom he was particularly close to. Both Curt and Lucas had European cars, but Lucas's was much sportier. Curt's college attendance is supported by the local Moose Lodge, being represented in the script by the owners of a small business. Lucas's studies at USC were paid for by his businessman father. What should one make of the fact that Curt helps the Pharaohs to rob the business of the people who support him?

13 Ravalli (2007: 1698) points out that Lucas's childhood address is often wrongly given as 530 Ramona Avenue. Additional references to Lucas's and to Coppola's biographies in the film include the number plate of John Milner's car ('THX 138') and the screening of Coppola's 1962 feature *Dementia 13* at the downtown cinema.

14 On teen-oriented films of the 1950s and early 1960s, see James (2017: 23–91), Brode (2015: 1–135), Klein (2011: 100–37), Tropiano (2006: 17–85), Doherty (1988) as well as McGee and Robertson (1982: 18–96). On teen-oriented music, see Hall (2014: 1–68) and Altschuler (2003: 3–160).

15 This paragraph and the next are based on Jones (2016: 141–59), Taylor (2016: 110–3, 126), Kaminski (2008: 37–9), Rinzler (2007: 7), Rubin (2006: 48–50), Hearn (2005: 55–71), Smith (2003: 33–44), Schumacher (2000: 146–7), Baxter (1999: 123–39, 147) and Pollock (1990: 108–23).

16 .On the special efforts made by sound designer Walter Murch to 'worldize' the music, that is to make it part of the diegetic world, see Beck (2016: 154–9). Also see Murch's many references to *American Graffiti* in Ondaatje (2002), esp. p. 119.

17 In addition, there is the enormous success of Don MacLean's single and album *American Pie* (both released in autumn 1971 and ranked third in the respective end-of-year US sales charts for 1972; Cader 2000: 220, 224). The song took an emotionally charged look at changes from the rock 'n' roll era to the early 1970s, referenced 1950s music and events – such as the death of Buddy Holly – which were also central to *American Graffiti*, and even prefigured the wordplay in the film's title.

18 This paragraph as well as the next one is based on Taylor (2016: 113, 126), Rinzler (2007: 7), Rubin (2006: 48–9), Smith (2003: 43), Schumacher (2000:

146–7), Baxter (1999: 135–9, 148), Jenkins (1998: 34–6), and Pollock (1990: 118–21).

19 Some sources (e.g. Hearn 2005: 71; Pollock 1990: 121) claim that the film was shortened by four and a half minutes. The *Variety* review of the film gives its length as 109 minutes (Murphy 1973: 20), whereas the *Daily News* and the *New York Times* give it as 110 minutes (Carroll 1973: 45; Greenspun 1973: 21); this suggests that the actual length was halfway between 109 and 110 minutes. The current version is 112 minutes and 30 seconds long. So it would seem that about 3 minutes were cut. The cuts included three scenes: encounters between Steve and a former teacher at the school dance, and between Terry and a car salesman as well as Falfa singing 'One Enchanted Evening' to Laurie (Smith 2003: 37, Baxter 1999: 138–9). As these three scenes are 2 minutes and 20 seconds long, there must have been further minor edits.

20 See http://www.impawards.com/1973/american_graffiti_ver2.html.

2 The Structure, Character Arcs and Themes of *American Graffiti*

The film begins in silence with the Universal logo emerging slowly. First, there is the star-filled sky, then the globe and three lines of text being superimposed on it: 'Universal', 'An MCA Company', 'Presents'. Almost immediately after the final image has taken shape, the film's silence is disrupted by radio sounds indicating that someone – somewhere on that globe – moves the dial in search of a station. The film cuts to a title card with green text on a black background: 'A Lucasfilm Ltd/Coppola Co. Production'. This image is accompanied, on the soundtrack, by a radio station jingle (for Mexico-based XERB which was the main station broadcasting Wolfman Jack's show from 1965 to 1971, while the DJ was living, and recording his programme, in the US, mostly in Los Angeles), the station being identified with the film production companies, and the station's programme which will play from then on with the film itself. Even before the film introduces its setting and characters, it positions the audience as radio listeners. Viewers are primed to pay special attention to the music and words about to be broadcast, and yet, just like the characters in the film, they are likely to perceive the radio programme mainly as a sonic backdrop (in fact, the film's characters only occasionally pay close attention to the broadcast).

With the next cut (26 seconds into the film), the jingle gives way to 'Rock Around the Clock', which plays over an extreme long shot (in fact a still image) of a Mel's Drive-In diner, the sign on the right side of the frame indicating that this branch is called 'Burger City'. It is early evening, the clouds are coloured red and the diner is brightly lit. There is only one car parked in front of it (near the centre of the frame), and a young man (who turns out to be Steve) leans on it. Bill Haley starts singing: 'One, two, three o'clock, four o'clock, rock'; his emphatic vocalisation of the word 'rock' is followed by the film's title being superimposed on the still image: 'American Graffiti', the words

DOI: 10.4324/9781315545509-3

looking a little bit like they were scrawled across the screen, thus mirroring the fake-handwritten lettering of the 'Mel's Drive-In' sign on top of the building and resonating with the very meaning of 'graffiti' (see Figure 2.1).

The design of Mel's Drive-In (as well as the chain's whole history since the opening of the first restaurant in 1947 and its rise to dominance of the Californian drive-in diner market in the 1950s)[1] and of the car in its parking lot (a '58 Chevy Impala) evoke the 1950s as does the song by Bill Haley and His Comets. 'Rock Around the Clock' serves as a potent marker of the beginning of the rock 'n' roll era, an era focused on teenage tastes and buying power (with regards not only to records but also, for example, to cars and the food and drinks served at places like Mel's Drive-In) as well as public concerns about juvenile delinquency. This sets up distinct expectations for the story and filmic experience to follow, to do with the 1950s and early 1960s (the latter being foregrounded in the film's tagline that most viewers would be familiar with), with classic rock and pop songs, teenagers and their elders, cars and places of consumption, fun and rebelliousness.

While the initial positioning of the audience as radio listeners and the powerful impact of 'Rock Around the Clock' suggest that the film offers a fully immersive experience of the past, its title complicates the picture. Universal had had serious concerns about 'American Graffiti' and considered many alternatives (Hearn 2005: 60). Interestingly, none of the contemporary reviews and articles I examined commented

Figure 2.1 Fake hand-written lettering in the film's title and in the first setting of its story.

on the film's title; it appears to have been accepted without question. The marketing of the film playfully acknowledged the fact that its title might sound odd to many people. In the trailer, Wolfman Jack says: 'American Graffiti – baby, what's that?' 'It's a movie!', comes the answer. According to the Oxford English Dictionary, the words 'graffito' (singular) and 'graffiti' (both singular and plural) since the early 1960s have referenced contemporary culture – '[w]ords or images marked (illegally) in a public place, esp. using aerosol paint' – and, ever since the 19th century, have referred to traces of everyday life in the ancient world: '[a] drawing or writing scratched on a wall or other surface; a scribbling on an ancient wall, as those at Pompeii and Rome'.[2] Either way, the title 'American Graffiti' suggests a certain detachment from, rather than full immersion in, the American way of life and culture on display in the film. Graffiti, in the original sense of the word, had to be unearthed and studied by archaeologists, and, in the contemporary meaning, they were nothing more than fragments of, or symbols for, a wider (youth) culture. Thus, the film's opening is characterised by a tension between immersion and detachment.

Back to the shot discussed above: Haley continues singing over the still image of Mel's Drive-In, and when he comes to 'We're gonna rock around the clock tonight', the film's title fades away to be replaced by the names of four cast members (in alphabetical order), all male. Next, come the names of three female cast members which suggests that the film revolves around three couples and an unattached male. The listing of the main cast ends with 'And Wolfman Jack', which reinforces the expectation that the audience will listen to a radio broadcast.

More credits follow, and they and 'Rock Around the Clock' continue when, at 1:22, the film finally cuts away from the still image to Terry arriving at Mel's Drive-In on a Vespa scooter (in what turns into another extreme long shot). He drives past Steve whose eyes follow Terry's movement for a moment, and who a few seconds later briefly turns around when Terry loses control of his scooter and crashes into a wall. Terry may be the kind of person who attracts attention mainly with his inept behaviour. The film cuts to another part of the diner's parking lot, where Curt arrives in his Citroen 2CV (in yet another extreme long shot). Once he is out of the car, he kicks it. While Steve comfortably leans on his stylish and expensive car, Curt shows contempt for his unattractive, cheap (and foreign) vehicle and Terry neither has a car nor does he even confidently command his scooter. Whereas the difference between Steve's and Terry's vehicles probably has to do with class (the latter simply not having the money to buy a car), Curt's French car is more likely to signal a somewhat bohemian attitude, which is also suggested by his attire, with the shirt hanging loose rather than being tucked in, the ensemble being completed by jeans and sneakers.

Continuing the shot of Curt's arrival, the panning camera follows him as he walks towards the diner and the final credits appear: 'Written by George Lucas and Gloria Katz & Willard Huyck' and 'Directed by George Lucas' (see Figure 2.2). As the only person in the shot during these credits, Curt is therefore closely associated with the film's co-writer and director. In fact, one might go as far as saying that Curt's small, foreign car and casual dress detach him from the more formal, and decidedly American, provincial culture of the past, situating him closer to the cosmopolitan, big city life of the early 1970s.

'Rock Around the Clock' comes to an end and the final credit fades away (it is gone by 1:59), while, still in the same shot with the camera following his movement, Curt arrives at Steve's car and Terry starts talking to him. Even before this first dialogue, the song's lyrics have indicated the film's story: a group of friends ('we') is having, or trying to have, fun 'around the clock', that is for about 12 hours. Indeed, as a repeated line insists, they are 'gonna rock, rock, rock 'til broad daylight'. We can expect that the story will end the next morning.

The shots featuring the studio logo and credits do a lot of expository work, introducing characters and a key setting of the story as well as suggesting a number of themes and a time frame. The film's exposition, or set-up, will continue for another eight minutes at Mel's Drive-In (ending at 10:09), introducing two more central characters

Figure 2.2 The filmmaker and the protagonist side by side: George Lucas and Curt Henderson.

– Laurie and John – and presenting a number of problems that the five protagonists will have to address in the course of the story. The film's development section, in which they work towards solving these problems, mostly while moving around and interacting with various people beyond the initial group of five, lasts until 81:31. The resolution, which sees the main characters briefly returning to Mel's Drive-In (but not all at the same time) before going off to Wolfman Jack's radio station (Curt) or to the climactic race at Paradise Road (the other four) – both locations being placed just outside town – shows how one after the other comes to terms with their issues. An epilogue (starting at 107:38) then reunites, for the first time since the exposition at Mel's Drive-In, all five protagonists; they are gathered at the airport the next morning, saying goodbye to Curt who departs for the East Coast, with captions superimposed on the blue sky relating what has happened to the four male characters by 1973. After the captions fade away, the credits start rolling.

The overall structure of the film can be represented as follows:

I   Set-up 0:00–10:08 (duration 10 min 8 sec): Mel's Drive-In (with credits), preceded by logo
II Development 10:08–81:31 (duration 71 min 23 sec): all around town, including returns to Mel's Drive-In, and near the canal just outside town
III Resolution 81:31–107:38 (duration 26 min 7 sec): Mel's Drive-In as well as the radio station and Paradise Road just outside town
IV Epilogue 107:38–112:22 (duration 4 min 45 sec): airport and blue sky, plus captions and credits

In this chapter, I first analyse the film's set-up, then its development and resolution before, in the chapter's conclusion, taking a close look at its epilogue.

Set-up

The film's first lines of dialogue, delivered, as already noted, by Terry (from 1:59 onwards), are: 'Hey, what do you say, Curt? Last night in town, you guys gonna have a little bash before you leave?' As Terry refers not only to Curt, but to 'you guys', and the only other person present is Steve, it can be assumed that both Curt and Steve are meant to leave the next day. Like his scooter and his somewhat awkward appearance (especially his glasses and perpetually open mouth) and behaviour (the scooter crash), Terry's dialogue lines set him apart from Curt and Steve. For whatever reason (in fact, he still has a year of school ahead of him), he is not going to leave the next day, nor has he been informed about, and included in, Curt and Steve's plan for their last night in town, the plan being, as it soon turns out, to attend the dance for new and returning pupils at their former high school (the Freshman Hop). Terry appears to be a friend of Curt and Steve's, but not a very close one.

Before Curt can answer Terry's question, Steve takes over the conversation (such sidelining of Terry will happen repeatedly): 'The Moose have been looking for you all day'. Only then do we get our first closer view of the characters, when (at 2:05) the film cuts to a medium shot of Curt, Terry and Steve. The following dialogue reveals that Steve's odd statement refers to the fact that the Moose Lodge has issued a $2,000 cheque for Curt so as to support his studies with its first-ever scholarship. Once again, Curt is marked as special; presumably he is an academically very gifted student who the local establishment thinks should be supported.

As Curt could not be found, the cheque was given to Steve who now hands it over to Curt, who is not at all happy about this and tries to hand it back. (Terry's interjection 'I'll take it', which playfully suggests that he is in need of money, is ignored.) The conversation is interrupted by a car honking, and the film cuts to Laurie who waves at the three young men and parks a '58 Edsel family car next to Curt's. Steve wants to walk over to her, telling Curt: 'your sister calls'. The demands of his girlfriend are more important to him than his conversation with Curt. But in the next shot, a close-up of the three young men which is followed by more close-ups from different angles, Curt demands that Steve first hears him out. Instead of leaving town the next day for a college in the East, he considers attending the local college for a year before he departs. Steve responds angrily, calling him a 'chicken fink' who, instead of getting out of 'this turkey town', wants 'to crawl back into your cell'. This is the first clearly defined issue. For the remainder of the film, one of the guiding questions is whether Curt will or will not leave town the next morning.

Immediately after Steve's line about voluntary imprisonment in their home town, a car engine roars off-screen, and the young men look towards the source of the sound, which a cut reveals to be a '32 Ford deuce coupe that has been transformed into a powerful racing car. The beginning of the shot is accompanied by Steve's next line of dialogue: 'You want to end up like John? You just can't stay 17 forever'. Since the age of majority (when a person acquires the legal status of an adult) is 18, Steve implies that John is an adult who is refusing to act his age, behaving like a juvenile instead. John is thus introduced in the film as a warning about the dangers of staying put.

The conversation between Steve and Curt ends with the latter's declaration, 'I just need some time', while the former twice says: 'We're leaving in the morning'. This phrase, as well as Steve's highly emotional response to Curt's doubts, suggests some insecurity on Steve's part: perhaps he, too, has doubts about leaving town, and he certainly does not want to do so on his own, requiring Curt's company on this adventure. There is also a potential conflict between Steve's insistence on their departure and the fact that he apparently is at Laurie's beck and call; in fact, all this time she has been sitting in her car, waiting for Steve to come over and open the door for her. He does so, and they embrace. As there is no mention of Laurie leaving town with Curt and Steve (because, like Terry, she has another year to go at school), there appears to be a very good reason for *Steve* to stay. Before this first scene of the film (which has been accompanied by low-level radio sounds) ends, the radio soundtrack gets louder and Wolfman Jack announces: 'We're gonna rock and roll ourselves to death'. This line suggests that there may be a lot at stake in the decisions the young people have to make about their future, and in the fun they are going to have during the night.

The second scene (starting at 3:34) opens with an extreme long shot of Mel's Drive-In similar to the one shown earlier, but now it is getting dark, and the bright lights of the diner make it stand out from the surrounding darkness. The parking lot is full, and cars are coming and going. The soundtrack features 'Sixteen Candles' (The Crests, 1958) about a girl's sixteenth birthday, sung by the young man who loves her and is 'wishing that you love me, too'; this could be understood as a reference to how Steve related to Laurie about a year earlier when she turned 16. A closer shot reveals waitresses on roller skates delivering trays to cars, the mobile camera following them. A medium close-up then shows John and Curt laughing and pretend-fighting, the latter exclaiming: 'Will you stop it with the Big Bopper stuff'. This is the first of two references to famous rock 'n' rollers in the dialogue, here relating to one who died (together with Buddy Holly) in a plane crash in 1959. By likening John to the Big Bopper, Curt suggests that he is a bit of a star (at least in this town) but there is also a hint at his mortality.

Echoing the way Steve and Curt were earlier distracted by the arrival of Laurie's car, Curt and John stop fooling around when a car honks off-screen. A cut reveals a vehicle full of young women, one of whom waves at and calls out to John, confirming that John is indeed well-known and popular. However, neither he nor Curt are impressed. Articulating his romantic frustration, Curt asks: 'Why is it every girl that comes around here is ugly, or has a boyfriend? Where is the dazzling beauty I've been searching for all my life?' This introduces a secondary issue for Curt to work through in the remainder of the story. He might or might not meet such a beauty during the night, and this will help him decide whether to stay or to leave the next morning.

John (the camera staying in a close-up on him for 20 seconds) says, 'I know what you mean', implying that he has been unsuccessful in his search for romance as well, but then takes Curt's statement in a new direction: 'The pickings are really getting slim'. This suggests that he is not so much looking for a romantic relationship than for sex with changing partners and that he has been doing this for a while with less and less success. Perhaps this is the behaviour Steve was referring to when he implied that John has refused to grow up – yet Steve, as will soon be revealed, tries to convince Laurie that growing up can mean having more than one romantic or sexual relationship at a time. John then takes the 'slim pickings' of possible sex partners as an indication of a general decline in the town's nightlife: 'The whole strip is shrinking'. He fondly remembers how much time and gasoline it took 'about five years ago' to complete a circuit on the town's crowded streets (as John implies that he was already driving then, his remark confirms that he is substantially older than the others). Wistfully, he concludes: 'It was really something'. He is remembering, and longing for, a different and better time, which once again appears to confirm Steve's earlier judgement (while also directly addressing the position viewers find themselves in, looking back from the 1970s to 1962 just as John is looking back from 1962 to the 1950s).

Right after 'something', an engine can be heard revving off-screen but instead of showing the car in question, the film cuts to Curt and then back and forth between him and John. Curt points out that the revving of what appears to be a new car in town implies a challenge to John and asks: 'Are you gonna go after him?' John mocks both Curt (who he addresses as 'professor' while pointing out that he has just asked a stupid question) and his challenger: 'If he can't find me, then he ain't even worth racing'. This establishes John as the fastest drag racer in town who other racers will want to challenge; he is a 'big shot', as Curt smilingly calls him, with regards to both fast cars and girls.

The exchange sets up a series of concrete questions to do with John's adventures during the forthcoming night: Will he find a young woman to have sex with? Will he eventually meet and beat his latest challenger? Will he come to terms with the fact that his experience of nightlife is not as satisfying as it used to be and that he might be too old for it? This last question mirrors an issue Curt and Steve have to deal with:

what if their future life in the East is not going to be as satisfying as the life they have now in their home town; what if they are not ready (that is, too young) for leaving?

The next dialogue (shown in close-up in one long take, lasting almost two minutes but being briefly interrupted by a cut-away to Terry running after Budda, one of the waitresses) shows Steve and Laurie sitting in her car, with her eating French fries and both looking towards the front of the car rather than at each other. Steve is a bit nervous and hesitant, asking Laurie twice to remind him how far he got with the little speech he has prepared. She remarks that he was 'leading up to something kind of big' to do with his love for her. Steve says that 'we should really consider ourselves as adults now' and that therefore they could agree on something before he leaves. There is a brief smile on Laurie's face which signals her expectation that this agreement has to do with them getting engaged. But what Steve wants her to agree to is that 'seeing other people while I'm away can't possibly hurt', that in fact 'it would strengthen our relationship'. Laurie is taken aback, but she is trying to hide her dismay by agreeing with everything he has just said. Perhaps she does not want to appear too needy which might put her in an even more disadvantageous position. But in order to remind Steve of the implications of what he is proposing she takes off the necklace which is a token of their relationship: 'it's juvenile now'; this indicates that she might end their relationship altogether (see Figure 2.3). Steve is not too happy about this, but when she adds, 'I can't expect you to be a monk or something while you're away', he seems quite (self-)satisfied.

Figure 2.3 Laurie is both upset and composed, after she has taken off the necklace Steve had given her.

This dialogue sets up questions for the two characters: How will Laurie deal with Steve's plan which she is clearly not happy about (presumably she was not happy about his imminent departure even before he came up with this plan)? Will she learn to accept it, or will she split up with Steve, or will she find a way to change his mind? Will Steve fully realise what he is proposing (which includes the possibility that Laurie goes out with other men and that he might lose her), and what will this realisation do to his plans for the future?[3]

A long shot shows Terry still pursuing Budda and being roundly rejected. Curt joins his sister (the camera being closer to the characters again), who is sitting alone in her car. He senses that something is wrong and asks her about it, but she refuses to discuss the matter. Meanwhile, Steve has joined Terry to tell him that he can have his car while he is away. He tries to give him some instructions, but Terry is so overwhelmed that he does not listen. Curt observes all this smilingly: 'Are you crying?' Terry is indeed deeply moved and declares: 'I'll love and protect this car until death do us part'. This line resonates across the whole film, echoing Wolfman Jack's earlier use of the word 'death' and Curt's reference to the Big Bopper. It refers back to the engagement and subsequent marriage that Laurie thought Steve's speech was leading up to and emphasises that young men may be more invested in objects than people, or rather that they become invested in objects precisely because human relationships have failed them. It is soon revealed that Terry thinks that temporary ownership of Steve's car will finally allow him to get some romance and/or sex into his life. The line also evokes the mortal danger associated with cars.

With new-found confidence, Terry asks Budda to come to a drive-in movie theatre with him. She laughs because she knows that he only has a scooter. At the very moment that he proudly declares that he actually has a car, John humiliates him by pulling down his trousers. Curt, Laurie, Steve and John all join in Budda's laughter. But, remarkably, Terry takes this in his stride, inviting Curt to join him for a ride in Steve's car. For the first time mentioning Terry's derogatory nickname ('Toad'), Curt declines the offer because he wants to go to the 'hop' with Steve and Laurie. He points out that 'I'd spoil your luck', referring to Terry's now presumably dramatically increased chances to get together with a girl. Terry declares: 'Tonight, things are gonna be different'. He is apparently used to being humiliated or ignored even by his friends and by the young women he approaches. Having been given Steve's car raises the question whether his romantic/sexual quest during the night will be successful, and whether he might be able to get more respect from people in general. This is connected to the fact that, with Curt and Steve scheduled to leave the next morning, Terry is bound to lose two friends from his day-to-day life, and he does not appear to have many more, with John being all too willing to denigrate him. Terry does need new social connections.

There is one more issue being raised in this scene. John reacts negatively and indeed angrily to Curt's plan to go to the hop with Steve and Laurie, especially after Curt declares (not altogether seriously) that 'we are going to remember all the good times' and invites John to come along. There are many possible reasons for John's forceful response. Perhaps he simply did not have a good time at high school (in fact, he is a drop-out). In addition, he is simply too old for the hop: 'That place is for kids'. Of course, Steve's earlier comment about John suggested that he behaved as if he wanted to stay 17 forever which would make it wholly appropriate for him to go to this high-school dance. However, John appears to have a keen sense of what is, and is not, age-appropriate behaviour; in fact, his angry reaction might indicate his awareness of the fact that people like Steve think that he has refused to grow up properly.

Curt's plan to go to the hop thus excludes John. As their earlier dialogue suggested, they are close, if somewhat unlikely, friends (the young intellectual and the older drag racer). John is not only disappointed that Curt apparently does not want to spend his last night in town with him, but is, on a deeper level, simply sad that he is leaving town. This echoes Laurie's (presumed) sadness regarding Steve's departure and also Steve's angry response to Curt's revelation that he might not leave town with him; Steve needs Curt to go with him just as John would prefer it if Curt could stay. John shouts: 'You go on over there and you remember all the good times you won't be having. I ain't going off to some goddamned fancy college!' In John's view, the pertinent point is that Curt is going to depart, leaving John behind. Curt's new, privileged life at a 'fancy college' thousands of miles away is going to contrast both with his present existence and, very sharply, with John's life in their home town. John almost screams: 'I'm staying right here! Having fun, as usual'. The implication is that there will be nothing 'usual' about it, because Curt will be gone.[4] (This exchange has implications for the viewers' position vis-à-vis the film: remembering one's past is fraught with complications, because one has to acknowledge that the 'good times' are irretrievably gone, and one may have to deal with events that were not 'good' at all.)

Curt does not get defensive, nor does he make a joke about the situation; he is genuinely concerned about John, who has walked away from the group to sit in his car (in a medium close-up). Curt goes over

to him: 'Did I do something wrong? I'm sorry'. He indirectly acknowledges that it might be his going away which causes John's distress.
John has calmed down and is perhaps embarrassed about his emotional outburst, looking away from Curt. Curt assures him that 'we'll
all do something together, you know, before Steve leaves'. John immediately realises that what Curt is saying is that he will not leave the
next morning, and he turns to look at him again. John is *not* pleased,
presumably because he is not thinking about himself at this moment,
but about his friend. He seems to assume that going away is the right
thing for Curt to do, and he wants the best for him. Asked directly
whether he is indeed not going to leave, Curt responds: 'I don't know'.
John exclaims 'Jesus' and drives off.

With this emphatic restatement of the main question that Curt has
to deal with, and of the more general theme of how the relationships
between friends and lovers are affected by life-changing decisions to be
made after the end of high school, the set-up ends (at 10:08). The night
that follows has been introduced as a rite of passage for these young
people in which they will come to (re)define who they are or want to
be, and how they relate to others. The next time any of the main five
characters are shown they have all left Mel's Drive-In behind.

Development

In less than two minutes, the development section catches up with all
the main characters, driving around town, and it does so in a particularly dynamic fashion. It is not just the case that characters and their
cars are mostly in motion (except for the short periods when they stop
at traffic lights or park somewhere), but the camera is moving almost
constantly as well. The development section starts with a crane shot,
the camera rising above a car-filled street (see Figure 2.4). This is followed by extreme long shots of the street, the camera usually panning
slowly. At other times, the camera is in front of cars in motion, or moving alongside them, showing characters in two cars looking at, and
talking to, each other in medium shots. The camera is also placed inside moving cars, especially when two or more characters interact in a
series of medium close-ups, with the outside world moving past in the
background. Camera mobility and fast editing in conversation scenes
are in line with the overall narrational strategy of cutting between several storylines; at all levels, the film is characterised by rapid change.

For the first three minutes of the development section, the film
switches quickly between storylines. After providing overviews of the
town's traffic (from 10:08 onwards), the film picks out John's car from

Figure 2.4 The film's main setting: streets crowded with cars.

the traffic and shows him in conversation with another driver who tells him about the challenger looking for him and about a police car at Jerry's Cherries (the implication being that the police are trying to catch drivers in illegal acts), before cutting (at 11:06) to Terry driving around in Steve's car and receiving abuse from people in other cars (one young driver calls 'what a waste of machinery', while a passenger in another car bares his butt). Next (at 11:45) Laurie's car is shown with her, Steve and Curt inside. At a traffic light, Curt exchanges looks with a blonde woman in a Thunderbird who appears to say 'I love you' to him (see Figure 2.5); Curt demands that they pursue her car but Steve and Laurie refuse.

This is followed by John's next scene (at 13:18), in which he decides to pursue a car full of young women and gets one of them (who he does not initially see) to join him in his car. Carol refuses to tell him exactly how old she is but is clearly too young. This comparatively long scene (almost three minutes) is followed by two scenes (adding up to two minutes) that feature Terry, the first of which (starting at 16:07) shows him getting into a minor accident when inadvertently reversing into the car behind him, while in the second (from 16:58) he is hassled by a car salesman.

These scenes can be grouped together as the first sequence of the development section. The sequence does not have much to say about how Steve and Laurie's relationship develops but it shows how Terry's attempt to improve his status with the help of Steve's car backfires,

Figure 2.5 Curt is confronted with an unknown woman who appears to say 'I love you'.

which seems to set him up for a long series of disappointments during the night. However, his absurd claim that the accident was the other driver's fault ('I won't report you this time') actually puts him in control of the situation and shows that he can handle himself under pressure. Curt's fleeting encounter with the kind of woman he said he had been searching for launches him on an open-ended pursuit. The sequence also confirms that John's search for 'fun as usual' is going to entail a race with his latest challenger and the search for a sexual partner, with the latter being derailed by Carol's age.

By paying attention to locations and the main storylines being followed, more sequences can be identified in the development section, each made up of several scenes, so as to arrive at the following segmentation:[5]

II.1 10:08–18:07 (9 min 59 sec): John, Terry, Steve & Laurie and Curt on the streets (in the order of their first appearance)

II.2 18:07–26:11 (8 min 4 sec): Laurie, Steve and Curt at the high school

II.3 26:11–33:01 (6 min 50 sec): John and Terry on the streets

II.4 33:01–38:14 (5 min 13 sec): Steve & Laurie and Curt at the high school

II.5 38:14–46:32 (8 min 8 sec): Terry, Curt and John at Mel's and on the streets

II.6 46:32–52:32 (6 min): Terry at a liquor store, John in a car junkyard

II.7 52:32–60:05 (7 min 33 sec): Curt, Steve & Laurie, John and Terry on the streets

II.8 60:05–71:38 (11 min 33 sec): Terry and Steve & Laurie at the canal, Curt at an arcade

II.9 71.38–81:31 (9 min 53 sec): John, Curt, Terry and Steve on the streets

With this segmentation in mind, it is now possible to follow the main storylines across the development section.

John spends all his time with Carol, never meeting any of the other four main characters during the development section. He first (in II.1) thinks he can get rid of Carol, and he then hides her presence from others because he is embarrassed to be seen with such a young girl; later on (in II.5) he tells people that he is baby-sitting his cousin. But he also takes care of Carol when, offended by his baby-sitting remark, she runs off into the street (also in II.5) and he subsequently bonds with her through conversations (especially in II.6) and joint action (an attack on another car in II.7).

Once Curt separates from Steve & Laurie (after II.1) he encounters a wide range of other people: his former teacher Mr. Wolf (in II.2), his ex-girlfriend Wendy (in II.4–5), three Pharaohs (in II.7–9) and two men running a local business (in II.8). But, despite several mistaken and actual sightings (in II.2, 5 and 7), he does not meet the mystery woman, nor does he get a conclusive answer to the question who she is: Wendy's friend Bobbie tells him that she is a rich man's wife (in II.5) while Joe, the leader of the Pharaohs, declares her to be a high-class prostitute (in II.9).

After a series of more or less unpleasant encounters with people in other cars, Terry (in II.3) finally manages to approach a 'bitchin' babe' (his words) on the sidewalk. Debbie responds positively to his comment that she looks 'just like Connie Stevens', then expresses interest in 'his' car and gets in (see Figure 2.6). For the rest of the development section, he spends all his time with her, having a run-in with an ex-lover of hers (in II.5), organising some liquor (in II.6), getting drunk and having sex near the canal, where Steve's car is then stolen from him (all in II.8). Afterwards (at the end of II.8 and the beginning of II.9), he briefly meets Steve, desperate to hide the truth about the stolen car both from him (who thinks the stolen car is Debbie's) and from Debbie (who does not know it belongs to Steve).

Steve has spent all his time up to this point with Laurie, arguing and then making up with her at the school dance (in II.2). They go on a romantic outing near the canal, which leads to a fight; she kicks him out of her car which he interprets as the end of their relationship (in

Figure 2.6 Terry manages to lure Debbie into Steve's car.

II.8). The couple is usually shown together during the development section (hence I sometimes refer to them as Steve & Laurie), but early on (towards the beginning of II.2) they are shown in separate lavatories, expressing very different views on their relationship to friends.

Thus, the storylines of John, Curt, Terry and Steve & Laurie do not intersect during the development section (except for Steve bumping into Terry after his separation from Laurie). Yet there are numerous other connections between the storylines, not least Wolfman Jack's radio programme which most characters are listening to most of the time – at one point (in II.7) they all comment on this show at the same time – and of course the fact that they are all spending most of their time sitting in, or standing next to, cars. In addition, characters in different storylines drive past each other (notably in II.7 and II.9) or converge on the same locations (Terry and John are at Mel's Drive-In in II.5, Terry and Steve & Laurie near the canal in II.8, Terry and Curt at Jerry's Cherries used car lot in II.9).

Visits to Mel's Drive-In tend to involve purchases of drinks and fast food. But (in II.5) Terry and Debbie drive off before their order is delivered, and Carol cannot finish drinking the coke John bought for her because they get into a fight. Instead of *spending* money at an arcade (in II.8), the Pharaohs break open the pinball machines to *get* money. Terry is unable to purchase liquor (in II.6), but eventually gets hold of a bottle and enjoys its consumption which in turn leads to sex with Debbie (and a severe bout of puking in the resolution). By contrast,

Steve & Laurie and Curt neither purchase nor consume goods during the development section. Overall, commercial exchanges play a surprisingly small role in it (in fact this applies to the set-up and the resolution as well).

John and his forthcoming race with Falfa are mentioned in conversations by Terry (bragging about his friendship with John when he first approaches Debbie) and by the Pharaohs (who think he is going to lose the race in II.7). Falfa approaches both Terry (in II.3) and John (in II.9). The police (mentioned in II.1) make appearances, in the person of Office Holstein, when hassling John (in II.3) and when (in II.9) becoming the target of a spectacular prank at Jerry's Cherries, this prank being executed by Curt and the Pharaohs, and witnessed by Debbie whereas Terry is too depressed to look up. Law (or rule) breaking is an element shared by all four storylines. Terry tries to get liquor although it is illegal for him to do so; after two failed attempts to purchase a bottle, it is finally handed to him by a man who is robbing the store and is then pursued by the gun-wielding owner (see Figure 2.7). In addition to the prank which wrecks the police car at Jerry's Cherries (see Figure 2.8), Curt covers for the Pharaohs when they rob the arcade, which, ironically, is owned by Hank Anderson who got the Moose Lodge to issue a cheque (shown in the set-up) to support his studies.

When Holstein stops John (in II.3), he accuses him of having done something illegal earlier that evening, but only writes him a ticket for the light on his license plate being out and promises to 'catch him

Figure 2.7 After finally getting a bottle of liquor Terry is stunned by the aftermath of a robbery.

Figure 2.8 The prank executed by Curt under pressure from the Pharaohs has a spectacular result.

in the act' at some point. Carol mentions a curfew that, apparently, applies to children her age, and which she is obviously breaking. By contrast, Steve and Laurie's only transgression is to dance too closely at the hop; when the supervising teacher Mr. Kroot interferes, Steve tells him to 'kiss a duck', and then laughs it off when Kroot tells him that he is 'suspended'. Across all four storylines, then, there are many instances of teenagers (and older youths like John, Joe and Falfa) being at odds with adults and their rules.

Indeed, there is an emphasis on people's age and life-stage in all the storylines, most obviously in the case of John (who is placed somewhere between extended adolescence and adulthood) and Carol (a child on the cusp of adolescence). Their different ages are used to indicate the rapid evolution of musical tastes; whereas Carol likes the newly popular Beach Boys, John hates 'that surfin' shit' and mournfully declares: 'Rock 'n' roll's been going downhill ever since Buddy Holly died'. Debbie seems so much more experienced, at least in sexual matters, that she might as well be much older than Terry, although in some respects she is surprisingly naive, perhaps childishly so, believing all the tall tales he tells her. Of course, they are both younger than 21 which turns the acquisition of liquor into such a drama. The mystery blonde Curt pursues has an air of maturity about her (and she may be married), which both echoes and contrasts with his former teacher Mr. Wolf's apparent romantic/sexual involvement with one of his pupils. Curt presumably finds sex with a somewhat older woman an attractive proposition but would not want to find himself as an adult having sex with school girls like Mr. Wolf (or indeed John). Steve sees the transition to college as a step up from his high-school relationship into the 'adult' world of changing sex partners ('we should really consider ourselves as adults'). Laurie, by contrast, sees her youthful feelings for Steve as the foundation of a life-long commitment.

In addition to age and life-stages, class and the world of employment are referenced in contrasting ways across the different storylines. Judging by their cars, dress and general demeanour Steve and Laurie appear middle-class, and there is no hint at them having to earn money by working. As Laurie's brother, Curt qualifies as middle-class as well (which suggests that he does not really need the money from the Moose Lodge) with a somewhat bohemian bent. By contrast, it is not only Terry's scooter which indicates that he comes from a less comfortable social background; during his attempts to buy liquor, he quickly runs out of money and has to get some from Debbie. John has a fancy car, but it is made clear (in a conversation with one of his regular customers in II.5) that he is a car mechanic, which indicates that the car is only as fancy as it is because he has been able to work on it himself. The fact that Debbie does not seem to own a car suggests – together with, for example, her platinum blonde bouffant hairdo – that she is working-class; she may well have a job but expects the boys she goes out with to pay for everything. It is unclear where to place Carol in all this although when John returns her to a nice home in the suburbs in the resolution, she definitely comes across as middle-class. Somewhat ironically, the mystery blonde may be a high-class 'working girl' or a rather bored (upper) middle-class wife (or even both?). Apart from her, the future prospects of characters appear to be tied to their class: while Steve and Curt have long been planning to leave town (and Laurie and Carol will no doubt have that option once they finish high school), John and Terry never even consider this possibility, nor do Budda or the Pharaohs.

Most fundamentally, there are parallels and contrasts between the four storylines to do with the relationships the main characters have established or want to establish. The four males are all basically looking for sex (with or without romance), while Laurie wants to maintain her romantic relationship (without intercourse). When apart from Steve in the girls' lavatory (in II.2), she tells her friend Peggy that she just wants to be with Steve, wishing she 'could go with him or something'; she certainly does 'not want to go out with any other guy'. Afterwards, she is clearly unhappy at the hop. The reasons should be obvious to

Steve (namely, their imminent separation and his plan to date other girls) but he ignores them and instead uses their subsequent romantic outing to pressure her into having intercourse; when she gives up her initial resistance, Steve does not want to proceed because she is unresponsive. He then provokes her with a remark about something she once saw Curt do (presumably he had sex), which makes her so angry that she kicks him out.

Curt wants to meet his dream woman, no doubt hopeful that this might lead to something sexual (and perhaps provide him with a good reason for staying in town), but instead bonds with Wendy and with the Pharaohs who eventually welcome him into their gang. Wendy kisses him dreamily and tells him that she is happy to hear that he is not going to leave town as planned, so that they can perhaps spend more time together. The motivation and intentions of the blonde woman in the Thunderbird remain, just like her identity, a mystery. In some ways, though, she comes across as a mirror image of John, Falfa and Mr. Wolf insofar as she seems to be on the lookout for younger sex partners.

Looking for casual sex, John is dealing with a young girl who freely talks about 'copping a feel', 'rape', getting 'a little action' and boyfriends, but is clearly not ready yet for any sexual interaction, at least not with someone so much older than she is. John uses this to trick her (at the very end of II.9) into revealing her address. It is not altogether clear why Carol is out that night in the first place. She was in a car with her sister, who presumably was meant to babysit her, but carelessly took her out for a night on the town with her girlfriends and then hands her over to what she fully knows is a man looking for sex. Without any justification, the older sister apparently places a lot of trust in John behaving properly towards Carol – which indeed he does.

At the beginning of the development section, one would expect that John will have no difficulties finding a willing sex partner and that Steve and Laurie will make the most of their final night together, while the chance of Curt finding his dream woman seemed rather slim and Terry's chance to have sex smaller still. And yet, while Curt never gets close to his dream woman, he does reconnect with his former girlfriend who seems eager to get back together with him, and Terry is the only one who appears to have fully satisfactory sexual relations.

While Terry is insecure, awkward and clumsy in his approach to Debbie, she does not only use her sex appeal to make him do things (like getting liquor) but also is straightforward about having sex. It is implied that she has had multiple lovers ('You seem to know a lot of weird guys', Terry observes). Her willingness, even eagerness to go all the way with Terry (which is what they do, it is implied if not actually shown) contrasts sharply with Laurie's reluctance to have intercourse with her long-term boyfriend. There is, as far as I can see, no critical judgement implied in this contrast: the film does not show Debbie's sexuality in a negative light, nor is Laurie condemned for being prudish. On reflection, one might, as a viewer, deduce that Laurie's behaviour (protecting her virginity) is guided by the sexual double standard subscribed to by middle-class youth, whereas working-class Debbie feels free to join the boys in having sexual fun.[6] (Indeed, from the perspective of the 1970s, Debbie could be seen as a harbinger of the sexual revolution.) But during a conversation at the school dance it is made clear that Laurie did much to initiate and develop her romantic relationship with Steve; she was not simply waiting for him to make a move.

The set-up has shown that for the five main characters sexual pursuits and romantic relationships are tied in with wider changes in their lives, with decisions about staying or leaving town, with the disruption of close social connections (to do with romance or friendship), and with reflections on what a good, and age-appropriate, life might look like. By the end of the development section, Steve's decision to leave town appears to have been confirmed by what he thinks of as his break-up with Laurie – although one can expect that once he fully realises his loss, he may have second thoughts. Conversely, Curt being welcomed by the Pharaohs and by his ex-girlfriend would seem to suggest that his doubts about leaving town, and his preliminary decision to stay, have been confirmed – and yet the fact that he is pursuing the elusive blonde indicates that he is looking for something extra, which perhaps his home town simply cannot give him.

For John, the development section revolves centrally around the appropriateness of his behaviour. As it turns out, driving for him is not only, or even primarily, about the thrill of competitive racing and the triumph of winning, but 'a serious business', even when just circling around town. Many things are simply inappropriate for a driver. So he is angry with Carol for squirting shaving cream in his face (in II.3): 'I ain't having no accident just because of you'. When Falfa embarks on a preliminary street race with him (in II.9) and wins because he crosses a red light, John declares him to be 'stupid'. And (in II.6) he wanders around among car wrecks, telling Carol about all the racers, as well as passengers and by-standers, killed in accidents. In a mixture of concern and admiration, Carol points out that he never had an accident; he responds: 'I came mighty close'. With regards to his driving, then, John is clear about what is, and is not, appropriate behaviour, and he is aware that nevertheless all his driving, and especially his racing, may well eventually result in a serious, perhaps lethal accident.

With regards to his pursuit of sex, John initially seems unreflective. When he approaches a car full of young women (in II.1) and attempts to lure one of them away, he lies about going to college. And when the high-school girl he is chatting up turns him down because she is going steady, he gives an almost self-mocking answer to her question whether it is okay that Judy's (at this point unseen) sister can join him instead: 'Judy, her sister, her mother, anybody. I take them all'. It is only fitting that the sister turns out to be too young for him. From then on, not only are references to sex or romance, mostly coming from Carol, exceedingly awkward for John, but he is also quite skillfully manoeuvred by her into the position of a caregiver. When he immediately announces that he will return her to her sister, she whines, asking whether she is 'too ugly', declaring that 'nobody wants me': 'even my mother and father hate me'. In response to her distress (which is partly an act, partly for real, it is difficult to tell for John), he is forced to start placating her, trying to make her feel better about herself and preventing her from doing something drastic (like screaming or telling the police that he tried to rape her).

Despite all the problems her presence brings him, he cannot simply accept her running away at Mel's Drive-In, not least because he suspects that she will not be safe on her own (and indeed a car full of young men starts following her). Retrieving Carol is a turning point; afterwards he opens up to her at the car junkyard, and when they are attacked with a water balloon that hits Carol in the face, he follows her guidance on how to take revenge: 'Just do what I say'. Stopping at traffic lights he deflates the other car's tires while Carol sprays its windows with shaving cream, both of them thoroughly enjoying themselves in what is arguably the most exhilarating scene in the whole film. In a subsequent encounter with Falfa, Carol relishes the insults John and his challenger exchange, and even joins in: 'Your car is uglier than I am'. Having tried and failed to get her to reveal her address before, at the very end of the development section John switches tactics, acting as if he was really drawn to Carol and no longer able to control himself – unless she tells him where she lives, which is what she does. This is accompanied by Johnny Burnette's 'You're Sixteen' (1960); 'You're sixteen, you're beautiful, and you're mine' are the final words of this scene, an ironic reminder of the male glorification of inappropriately young girls.

John's tricking of Carol concludes the development section. Having used a sexual scenario to manipulate Carol, and doing so for her own good, John will now be able to return her home and then confront his challenger unencumbered. The police who had been trying to catch

John in some transgression (such as an illegal car race) have been disabled by the prank Curt has executed for the Pharaohs, bonding with them in the process and presumably regaining his freedom for the rest of the night. Having surveyed much of what the town has to offer, he now is free to pursue the mystery woman again and to make a final decision about staying or leaving in the morning. Terry has seemingly won over Debbie but lost the car that helped him do so. His house of lies is crumbling and he does not appear to be able to keep up the pretence for much longer. Having been kicked out of her car by a very angry Laurie, Steve thinks that their relationship is over. But Laurie still has not told him that all along, more than anything else, she just wanted to be with him. As she is absent from the final scenes of the development section, it is unclear how she feels after her big fight with Steve, and he is only beginning to contemplate a life without her.

Resolution

In a repeat of the set-up, the first sequence of the resolution has the five main characters assemble at Mel's Drive-In, but not all at the same time. Steve, Laurie and Curt arrive at the beginning of the sequence, Terry and John at its end. The second sequence then introduces a clear spatial division, with Curt searching out the station from which Wolfman Jack broadcasts while the others gather for the climactic race:

III.1 81:31–95:56 (14 min 24 sec): Steve, Laurie, Curt, John and Terry at Mel's and on the streets
III.2 95:56–107:38 (11 min 42 sec): Curt at the radio station and at Mel's, Steve, Laurie, John and Terry at Mel's, on the streets and on Paradise Road

Harking back to the film's first shot of Steve standing next to his car in front of Mel's Drive-In, the resolution starts with a shot of Steve on his own, this time sitting inside the diner (see Figure 2.9). Budda, who is still at work, joins him and gets him to reveal that he and Laurie have broken up, which leads her to invite him to her place when her shift finishes (she takes the initiative just like Laurie did when she first got involved with Steve). At this moment (82:11), Laurie, who was last seen kicking Steve out of her car and driving off (at 69:18), appears on foot outside the diner. Perhaps she is returning to this meeting point to find Steve and to talk about what has happened. Two close-ups focus on her reaction to seeing Steve with Budda (see Figure 2.10). She does not seem to be surprised, turns around and walks away. The conversation

Figure 2.9 Steve is on his own again at Mel's.

Figure 2.10 Seeing Steve with another girl, Laurie is once again both upset
and composed.

between Steve and Budda then suggests that they have had some kind
of romantic/sexual history (which Laurie probably knows about).
'This time it will just be for fun', Budda says, and Steve half-heartedly
goes along. It seems that his fantasy of 'seeing other people' is coming
true. But he immediately changes his mind again: 'I just don't think it
would work out'. Apparently, he begins to realise that what he really
wants is his relationship with Laurie.

Next (at 82:55) Curt arrives in the Pharaohs' car, all of them still being excited about their prank and acting very chummy with each other, despite all previous tensions between them and their apparent differences in terms of class and ethnicity (see Figure 2.11).[7] Joe has plans for them for the next evening, but Curt is hesitant: 'I guess so, I don't know'. After more banter, the last thing he says is: 'See you, boys'. Perhaps he will stay in town, perhaps not. One of the deciding factors may well be his pursuit: 'I gotta find the blonde'. He walks to his car in a long take panning shot which reverses the one of him walking away from his car in the set-up. Sitting in his car he is then listening (in close-up) to someone dedicating a song on the Wolfman Jack show 'to keep me and my girlfriend together'; while Curt does not show any sign of recognising the voice, it very much sounds like Steve. When Wolfman Jack says 'I'll bring you right together', Curt sees the white Thunderbird, but cannot get his car started to pursue it. The coincidence of the DJ's promise and his latest sighting of the mystery blonde's car might have given Curt an idea of how he can reach her.

The song selected by Wolfman Jack starts to play, but when (at 84:47) the film cuts to a close-up of Laurie driving, with Falfa's car next to hers, its engine roaring, the song cannot be heard, which indicates that she did not hear (what presumably was) Steve's dedication. As the scene progresses, the song (The Skyliners' 'Since I Don't Have You', 1958) becomes clearly audible again: 'I don't have anything, since I don't have you'. All of this strongly implies that Steve really wants her back, but she is under the impression that he has already moved

Figure 2.11 Friendship across class and ethnic divides: Curt and the Pharaohs.

on to another girl. So she agrees to get into Falfa's car (taking over from various other women who have previously occupied it). She is not looking for sex or even just conversation: 'Don't say anything and we'll get along just fine'. She simply wants to be seen in Falfa's car, perhaps to declare her independence, or to retaliate against Steve, to make him jealous.

Next (at 84:47), John and Carol arrive in front of her parents' house. In medium close-up shot/reverse shots, Carol wants some confirmation from John: 'Do you like me?'; 'Couldn't I have something to remember you by?' She looks extremely vulnerable and needy (see Figure 2.12), and John just has to play along, giving her the gearshift knob she had been toying with before and kissing her quickly on the cheek. Her demeanour changes immediately; she is not only happy but assertive, even triumphant (see Figure 2.13): 'It's like a ring or something. It's like we were going steady. [...] Wait until I tell everybody about this'. She ignores John's objections, knowing she has outsmarted him. With a casual 'I see you around' she leaves the car and goes home. The scene ends with a long-held medium close-up of a thoughtful John.

Back at Mel's Drive-In (at 87:27), Curt is fixing his car while, echoing their conversation in the set-up and a conversation Steve had with Laurie (in II.8), Steve now doubts that it makes sense to leave friends to make new friends, etc., whereas Curt repeats lines he has heard from Steve all summer about 'leav[ing] the nest', exploring 'the big, beautiful world' and such. Reversing the conclusion of their conversation in the set-up, Curt now advises Steve to 'just relax': 'we will talk

Figure 2.12 Carol projects vulnerability and neediness to get what she wants.

Figure 2.13 Carol is triumphant after having manipulated John.

about it at the airport'. He wants both Steve and himself to have a little bit more time for making the final decision. Curt drives away for what he tells Steve is a 'dental appointment'.

After a brief reminder (from 88:27 to 89:00) of Laurie being in Falfa's car, with him singing 'Some Enchanted Evening' to her, Terry's storyline is picked up again. While loud puking noises can be heard, several adults look at what must be Terry's body (hidden behind a car) responding violently to the alcohol he has consumed. This is the low point of Terry's night, an exaggerated version of the incident in the set-up when John pulled down his pants in front of Budda and everyone else. Terry has lost Steve's car, makes a spectacle of himself before a group of strangers and shows himself in the worst possible light to Debbie. But Debbie takes this in her stride, holding on to the idea that Terry is used to drinking a lot because 'he told me so'.

When Terry finally emerges from behind the car, he discovers (at 89:50) that Steve's car is parked nearby and decides to 'steal it right back' by hotwiring it. This initiates a series of brief scenes going back and forth between John (leaving the garage where he works, driving on the street, seeing Terry) and Terry (being apprehended by the car thieves who then beat him up, with Debbie vigorously but ineffectively trying to help him by hitting them with her handbag). This culminates in John coming to the rescue, beating the car thieves and then making sure that Terry is alright. When he inquires whether Debbie, who is holding Terry, is 'with him', Terry declares: 'You're talking to the woman I love' (see Figure 2.14). All of this is partly played for laughs, but two serious points are being made: Debbie is really standing by Terry, who very much appreciates this, and, contrasting sharply with his humiliation of Terry in the set-up, John turns out to be a true friend when it really counts, taking a significant risk by confronting two strong, young men.[8]

The film next (at 92:36) returns to Steve, who is sitting alone in the diner as he had done at the beginning of the resolution. Once again someone joins him – now it is two girls from school who, in a round-about way, tell him that Laurie has joined Falfa in his car. The song 'Teen Angel' playing in the background is rather ominous in this context as it concerns a girl dying in a car accident. Shortly after Terry and Debbie (at 93:15) arrive at the diner in Steve's car, Steve comes out and takes his car back, presumably to try to find and confront Laurie.

Debbie is baffled by Terry's second loss of the car, and Terry has to come clean: 'It's not my car'. In response to her follow-up questions, he has to admit that he does not even own a car. Debbie is not angry with him for lying, but she does have a practical concern: 'How am I going to get home?' She walks away to ask someone else for a ride. For a moment, it looks like his rejection by Budda in the set-up is being replayed, but this time John, who is parked nearby, shows concern, rather than making fun of him. Then Debbie comes back and sits down next to him to tell him that she 'had a pretty good time tonight' because so many exciting events occurred (among them the 'hold-up' of the liquor store and a 'bitchin' fight'). One might consider this a case of instant

Figure 2.14 Terry can count on people who will stand by him.

nostalgia: Debbie fondly looks back at a night full of challenges and, judging that she and Terry mastered them all, she takes this as an inspiration for the future. She is ready for more, asks Terry to give her a call the next evening and kisses him goodbye on the mouth.

In the set-up, Terry was being ignored, rejected, humiliated and left to drive out into the night on his own, but in this first sequence of the resolution he is strongly supported and taken care of by Debbie and by John. Steve and Curt might both be leaving in the morning, yet Terry knows he can count on two other friends. He does not need a fancy car or tall tales for this; quite on the contrary, one might say that his vulnerability and his defeats (and his humour in the face of adversity) are the foundation for the bonds he forms with Debbie and John. Not least through his time with Carol, John has learnt to take care of people, acting to some extent how one might expect a responsible and dedicated older brother to behave. There is no indication that he will be chasing high-school girls again any time soon (however, there is no indication that he definitely will *not* do so either). And yet, despite all the danger, he is ready to race Falfa. Laurie is rather desperate, doing something very much out of character,[9] but the news of her riding with Falfa has managed to mobilise Steve, so that it may yet all be working out for her. And Curt, who started the evening in conversation with three friends and his sister, then left Mel's Drive-In in a car with Steve and Laurie, now drives off on his own, because he still has to find the mystery blonde – and make up his mind about the future.

The second sequence goes back and forth between, on the one hand, Curt's storyline revolving around Wolfman Jack and the mystery blonde, and, on the other hand, the storylines of Laurie, Terry, John and Steve which converge on the climactic race. Even though it is only at the very end of the sequence that Curt explicitly states that he is going to leave town, the separation of his storyline from those of his friends already strongly suggests this. In particular, his unwillingness to support John at a crucial moment sends a strong signal, as does his lack of interest in what has happened to his sister.

Curt has picked up on a comment made by the Pharaohs' leader Joe, who is countering all kinds of rumours about Wolfman Jack by pointing out that he is broadcasting from a station at the edge of town. Upon arriving there Curt is invited into the studio by a middle-aged man who claims *not* to be the Wolfman; he just puts on records and plays tape recordings of the DJ's patter (see Figure 2.15). While Curt wants to relay a message to the mystery woman, he gets drawn into a conversation about his future. He explains that the dedication has

Figure 2.15 Wolfman Jack plays a man who pretends he is not the Wolfman (but really is).

to be broadcast before the morning because 'I may be leaving town tomorrow'. The man encourages him to take the leap; he says that the Wolfman would tell Curt: 'Get your ass in gear [...] It's a great, big, beautiful world out there' (echoing the words Curt repeated in III.1 from the incessant commentary he had received from Steve during the summer). On the way out Curt realises that the man does not only play tapes but delivers the familiar patter. He is the Wolfman after all, and since he has said that he is stuck in this studio at the edge of town, his praise of the big, beautiful world is undermined, while his legendary status among the town's youth shows that much can be achieved without going away. It is not at all clear what Curt can take away from this for the decision he has to make.

While Curt returns to Mel's Drive-In, listening to Wolfman Jack telling his audience that a woman in a white Thunderbird should meet or call Curt at the phone booth in the diner's parking lot, John and Falfa arrange to meet for a race on Paradise Road. Terry joins John so that he can give the starting signal for the race, and Falfa rejects Laurie's request to get out of the car before the race. Steve finds out about the location of the race and tries to get there as fast as possible, knowing that Laurie is with Falfa. On Paradise Road, Terry steps out of John's car and prepares to give the signal, and John tells Laurie to get out of Falfa's car – but, although she has just demanded the same thing from Falfa, now she insists on staying. Steve is nowhere to be seen.

In some ways, ever since the first mention of a challenger in the set-up, the whole film has been building up towards this race. There has been plenty of talk about the forthcoming race, even a little test run between Falfa and John; there have been general references to the 'serious business' of driving, to drivers' carelessness and stupidity, to lethal accidents (in addition a non-lethal car accident has been staged as a prank). The town's youth seem to be invested in the outcome of the race, wishing the local hero to win against the challenger from out of town. At the same time, social interactions to do with friendship, sex, romantic love, caring or status have clearly been at the centre of the story. Indeed the importance of the climactic race derives partly from the opportunity it provides for Terry to take centre stage for one glorious moment through his association with John, from John's apprehensiveness about the dangers of driving and from the fact that Laurie puts herself in danger as well, with Steve racing to the rescue, as it were.

From the moment Curt arrives back at Mel's Drive-In (at 102:02) to the start of the race (at 103:30), the sky brightens (unrealistically quickly) from what previously had been a deep darkness to the dawn of a new day. The race is decided when Falfa's car veers off the road after only ten seconds. It catches fire and eventually explodes, but only after John has made sure that everyone keeps their distance from it, personally leading Falfa away (see Figure 2.16), while Steve, who has just arrived at the scene, walks off with Laurie. All shook up by the accident, she finally says what she had not been able to say before: 'Please don't leave me'. Having almost lost her, Steve makes a promise:

Figure 2.16 John gets Falfa away from his car before it explodes.

'I won't'. Despite John's observation that Falfa 'was pulling away from me just before he crashed', Terry refuses to acknowledge that John is not the fastest anymore: 'You'll always be number one'. John gives in and makes a kind of pact with Terry, standing next to his car and in front of the rising sun: 'We take 'em all'. Also in front of the rising sun, Steve and Laurie walk arm in arm towards the camera at the end of the scene (see Figure 2.17).

The beginning of a new day has brought definite resolutions for four of the main characters. After being separated from Laurie, hearing about her association with another man and witnessing the aftermath of the accident, Steve realises that more than anything else he wants to be with her, thus mirroring her feelings for him which, in the wake of risking and almost losing her life in the car race, she can finally tell him about. Terry does not only start the race but is graciously allowed by John to declare the winner and is then included in the 'we' that is going to face all future challengers together; this confirms their friendship and will most likely earn him some respect by profiting from John's special status in this town. Of course, to some extent this is based on a lie: John's car was not the fastest in this race, a fact that John finds very upsetting. But John realises that Terry, as well as many other young people in his home town, needs him to be the champion, and he agrees to continue playing this role. Instead of longing for the music, the nightlife and his racing prowess of the past, he looks to the future, together with a friend who, it is now clear, he will take care of in the same way that he took care of Carol.

Figure 2.17 Steve and Laurie are reunited as the new day begins.

But what about Curt? It is important to note that he is not needed for the resolution achieved by the others. While Steve and Laurie as well as John and Terry have helped each other, Curt has made no serious effort to help anyone (except, ironically, the Pharaohs) and in his last scene with Steve even encouraged him to depart for college in the morning and leave his sister behind. He did not keep his promise to John that they would do something together during the night. Instead, he has fallen asleep in his car, only to be woken up, after the new day has begun, by a phone ringing. His nighttime visions of the mystery blonde are now complemented by a daytime voice, which retains the woman's mystery; she does not reveal who she is or how she knows Curt but tells him that he can find her cruising Third Street that evening. It is only now that it becomes clear how Curt is going to resolve his issues: he will not pursue the mystery woman any longer because he is going to leave town that morning.

Whatever the woman – or indeed his home town as a whole, with his old friends and his new friends in the Pharaohs gang, his supporters in the Moose Lodge, his ex-teachers and his ex-girlfriend – could conceivably offer him, it is never going to be enough. After the woman says goodbye and Curt puts down the receiver, a smile appears on his face (see Figure 2.18), as if to indicate that this is, after all, a satisfying conclusion to his adventures: they have helped him decide what to do next. But it is also a very lonely moment. Unlike Steve and Laurie walking arm in arm into the new day and the 'we' of John and Terry looking forward to taking them all, Curt is alone and moves towards

Figure 2.18 Curt is at peace, happy with the decision to leave his home town.

the future on his own. He does not know it yet, but the audience does: even Steve will not be with him on his journey to the East.

Conclusion

In many ways, the film's epilogue returns to its opening sequence, bringing the five main characters back together again, and highlighting both the – romantic as well as non-romantic – pair bonds that have been strengthened in the course of the story (Steve and Laurie, Terry and John), and Curt's separateness. The scene starts (at 107:38) with an extreme long shot of the five main characters being joined by Laurie and Curt's parents. This is the only appearance of parents of one of the main characters in the film, and they are quickly being sidelined again so as to reiterate the film's almost exclusive focus on youth. In a long take medium shot (running from 107:47 to 109:01), Curt first says goodbye to his parents, then to Steve and Laurie (who may well grow into adulthood and middle age in Modesto together just like the parents did) and finally – with the camera following his movement – to Terry and John, before walking and then running towards the plane in the background, while John, Laurie, Steve and (mostly hidden) Terry stand in the foreground looking after him. A reverse medium long shot then shows his four friends and his parents waving to him. After a long shot of Curt waving back while stepping into the plane, the four other main characters are shown once again, this time in a medium close-up, which is held for five seconds so as to register the feelings playing on their faces: there is pensiveness, doubt, some sadness and even, in the case of John, frustration (see Figure 2.19).

With their final handshake, Steve has promised that he will join Curt in the East a year later, a promise he presumably will not keep. Terry has joked: 'Stay cool, man. And don't do anything I wouldn't do'. In the light of Terry's rather extreme experiences during that night, this amounts to saying something like 'Do it all'. But the most deeply resonant parting line comes from John, delivered with a light slap in Curt's face: 'You probably think you're a big shot goin' off like this, but you're still a punk'. With this statement, John acknowledges that the two friends are going their separate ways, and in a mock-aggressive way asserts that their bond cannot be broken, although it most likely will.

In terms of both content and style, this shot sequence (much like the film as a whole) moves from emphasising the togetherness of the five protagonists to emphatically staging Curt's separation from the others. Subsequent shots show the plane taking off in an extreme long shot and Curt, in close-up, being thoughtful and then looking

Figure 2.19 Conflicting emotions in the faces of those who have had to say
        goodbye to Curt.

out the window, where he sees a white Thunderbird driving across the
countryside deep down below, which appears to make him even more
thoughtful in a second close-up (see Figure 2.20). This dissolves into
the blue sky across which his plane (now only a tiny fleck in the image) flies and on which the captions are printed, while the faint sound
of the aircraft engine can be heard. It almost seems that what Curt
is contemplating in that final close-up is not just what has been hap-
pening that night and morning, but also the fate of his friends and his
own fate as displayed in the captions: John's death, Terry's disappear-
ance in Vietnam, Steve's continuation of his life in Modesto and Curt's
move to Canada. The implication is that Laurie lives with Steve, but
apart from this, the connections between the film's five protagonists
are shattered.

However, Curt becomes a writer who, from the point of view of 1973,
can – like writer-director George Lucas – look back on that morning
after the last night of summer when he said goodbye to his home town
and his friends, and also on that night and on the summer – and all of
their shared years – preceding it. It is wholly appropriate then that the
credits are accompanied by 'All Summer Long' (1964) by the Beach
Boys. With the oft-repeated line 'We've been having fun all summer
long', the song is about romance, sex, games, moving around, freedom
and 'thrills', and about all of this soon coming to an end: 'Won't be
long 'til summer time is through'. It is a celebratory and ever so slightly

Figure 2.20 Curt contemplates the past, present and future.

melancholic song about the (recent) past, the present moment and connections between the two – much like the film it concludes.

Notes

1 See https://melsdrive-in.com/about/ and http://kipsamericangraffiti.blogspot.
com/2012/08/mels-drive-in-true-story-of-worlds-most.html.
2 See https://www.oed.com/view/Entry/80475.
3 In the scene after the dialogue between Steve and Laurie, the song 'Gee'
(The Crows, 1954) is playing in the background, and while its lyrics can
hardly be heard, this is another, very subtle hint at future developments.
The lyrics emphasise a young man's devotion to the girl he loves: 'I'm not
takin' chances / because I love her, I love her so-o'.
4 The film is quite playful in suggesting the depth of John's feelings. He addresses Curt as 'Curtsy baby', which is a derogatory but also, potentially,
a loving term. After the end of this scene, John is shown driving around,
accompanied by the song 'Runaway' (Del Shannon, 1961) in which the
male singer mourns the loss of his lover who ran away: 'Wishin' you were
here by me, / To end this misery'.
5 As previously discussed, the set-up is made up of only one sequence (I.1
0:00–10:08), which includes the credits and consists of two scenes.
6 On middle-class sexual norms and practices in 1950s and early 1960s
America, see Breines (1992: 84–126) and Bailey (1994: 239–47).
7 It is important to note that while all the main characters of the film are
clearly white, the Pharaohs cannot be labelled quite so easily. One of
them is called Carlos, and there are references to Gil Gonzalez and Toby
Juarez who may or may not be additional members of the gang or friends

of theirs. The leader is called Joe, played by white actor Bo Hopkins but here appearing with a very deep tan. Overall one is inclined to identify them as Latinos. It could be argued that it probably fits the demographic profile of Modesto in the early 1960s to have Latino characters but, with the exception of a few couples at the school dance, no African Americans in the film. For a critical discussion of ethnicity and race in Lucas's early work, see Marez (2016: 119–42).

8 The song playing through most of this is 'Chantilly Lace' (1958) by The Big Bopper. In the set-up Curt likens John to this singer. Debbie here likens him to the Lone Ranger.

9 The risk Laurie takes when riding with Falfa echoes the story of another girl who got so upset after her boyfriend had joined the marines that she had a nervous breakdown and 'got run over by a bus', according to Laurie's friend Peggy who wants Laurie to calm down (in the bathroom conversation at the beginning of II.2).

3   The Marketing, Reception and Success of *American Graffiti*

The press book prepared by Universal for the release of *American Graffiti* in August 1973 described the film as 'director George Lucas' homage to his teen years' (Universal 1973: 1). 'Set in a small California town', the film's story is said to revolve around four male friends at a crucial point in their young lives: 'Tonight marks the end of the group, a break from their old lives' (ibid.). The press book prominently featured a list of the songs used in the film, which were said 'to represent the sentiments of the characters and also the hopes, dreams and absurd comedies of the beginning of the JFK-New Frontier – back when kids still looked at the world with awe and the music was sweeter' (ibid.). The reference to John F. Kennedy was double-edged, evoking both a sense of renewal in American society in the early 1960s and the shock of an abrupt ending caused by the assassination of the president in November 1963. The press book implied that after Kennedy's death the world had taken on a darker hue, and not just for 'kids'. This socio-cultural transition was mirrored in the story of *American Graffiti*, insofar as it pointed forward to new experiences awaiting the protagonists after the 'break from their old lives', but the film was also said to celebrate the life they had shared with each other before 'the end of the group'. According to the press book, then, endings and new beginnings characterised the stories of the film's protagonists and the society of the early 1960s in which they lived.

The press book hinted at new beginnings in the film industry, associated with a new generation of filmmakers. The film's 34-year-old producer, Francis Ford Coppola, was introduced as 'the best known whiz kid to come out of the cinema department of an American university' (Universal 1973: 4), with a long list of film credits as a writer, director and producer, most notably for *The Godfather*. As far as the press book was concerned, Lucas's credentials were less impressive: 'Lucas, 28 years old, was born and raised in Modesto, California. [...] Cars

DOI: 10.4324/9781315545509-4

and drag racing were his primary interests when he was growing up' (4–5). Rather than his previous film work (which is never mentioned), his main qualification for making *American Graffiti* appeared to be that he had lived the life that his film depicted. Presumably so as to bolster his standing as a gifted filmmaker, the press book added: 'but he was also an extremely able art student' (5). Overall, though, the emphasis was on the film's authenticity, rather than its artfulness, and the press book concluded with a note on Wolfman Jack. He 'came to fame during 1958–66', broadcasting from a secret location: 'No one knew anything about Wolfman for years and there was much speculation' (10). In addition to enhancing the film's claim to truthfulness by playing himself, Wolfman Jack, who, as noted above, by the early 1970s had become a highly visible celebrity, served as the film's main attraction.

The press book offered journalists various frames for writing about *American Graffiti*, so that their writing – like the film's advertising (discussed in the Introduction) – might in turn attract cinemagoers to the film and help them to engage with it productively. It is worth noting that the film's reviews often echoed the press book's main points, none more so than the one included in an information booklet issued by the National Council of Churches (1973), which used some of the very same language.

In the first section of this chapter, I outline the various stages of the release of *American Graffiti*, arguing that across its extremely long run the film's audience was mostly made up of educated baby boomers. In the second section, I use a range of reviews to explore how critics, and also perhaps those educated baby boomers, enjoyed and made sense of the film, whereas the third section relates the film's success to broader developments in American society, in particular to the experiences and outlook of the baby boom generation.

Marketing, Success and Audience Demographics

In the light of *American Graffiti*'s low production budget, it is not surprising that Universal's marketing budget for the film was quite small. The distributor spent only $500,000 on prints and advertising (p&a) (Baxter 1999: 148; Pollock 1990: 123), at a time when the average ad spending for a Hollywood movie – without the cost of making film prints, which usually made up between a quarter and a fifth of total p&a costs – was $890,000, most of this being used to pay for advertising in newspapers and magazines (Block and Wilson 2010: 417; Cook 2000: 493). Given the comparatively small amount of paid advertising for *American Graffiti*, the studio's ability to generate press interest in the film, that is free publicity, was particularly important.

It was therefore quite a coup for George Lucas to be interviewed twice by the *New York Times* in the months after *American Graffiti*'s release in August 1973. These interviews signalled both the considerable renown he had achieved as a young filmmaker, and how successful he and the studio had been in getting the press to pay attention to *American Graffiti*.[1] The resulting articles did not only direct the newspaper's readers' attention to a movie currently on release, but also allowed Lucas to highlight what he considered to be the most noteworthy and most appealing qualities of his film. In September, Lucas told the *New York Times* that *American Graffiti* dealt with dramatic changes the United States had undergone in recent times, and the effect this had had, and continued to have, on Americans: 'The early sixties were the end of an era. It hit us all very hard' (Gardner 1973: D40). Although Lucas emphasised that the film 'came entirely from his head' – that is, it was his creation – and was based on his own teenage experiences and informed by his own feelings ('I was angry and hurt'), he made it clear that he considered its story to be reflective of the experiences and feelings of 'us all'.

A few weeks later, Lucas once again told the *New York Times* that the film was both about himself and about all Americans: 'It all happened to me. [...] I [...] drove the cars, bought liquor, chased girls [...] I think a lot of people do, which is the whole idea behind the title – a very American experience' (Klemesrud 1973: D1). Lucas emphasised the continuities of American teenage life across the decades, pointing out that 'they still cruise a great deal, especially on Van Nuys Boulevard in Los Angeles' (D13). His film was thus dealing with a somewhat timeless youth experience, giving audiences access to a 'glamorized' version of the pleasures of young people's lives; it was 'designed primarily for fun, to be entertaining, [...] a warm movie about what it's like to be a teen-ager' (ibid.).

He also reiterated that the movie grappled with processes of historical change, past and present. *American Graffiti* was about an era 'coming to an end' in the 1960s: 'people have to change. [...] You have to go from a warm, secure, uninvolved life into the later sixties, which was involvement, anti-war stuff, evolution, and a different kind of rock 'n' roll' (Klemesrud 1973: D13). He added that '[n]ow we're changing again' (ibid.), which implied that looking back on the previous decade would help people to deal with the demands of the present. He pointed out that a lot could be learnt from teenagers, because, in any historical period, their particular stage in life was, more than later life-stages, about the difficulty of dealing with change, with new challenges: 'for a lot of kids, it's one of the hardest things to do in life, to plunge into something new' (ibid.). Watching how young people negotiated that plunge might provide encouragement and insight for everyone who had to confront a changing world. In these interviews, then, Lucas promoted his film as a highly enjoyable as well as a deeply meaningful experience.

Another marketing tool was the film's music. A soundtrack double album released by one of the major record companies (MCA Records, which belonged to the same media conglomerate as Universal) sold over half a million copies by the end of 1973 (Smith 1998: 173), continuing to sell extremely well in 1974 so that it became the sixth biggest selling album of that year (Cader 2000: 224). The record's success drew more attention to the film, enticing more people to watch it; and it prefigured one of the key experiences viewers were being offered by the film, namely, sensual immersion in the past. A similar effect was achieved by the activities of Wolfman Jack, who played music from the film, and talked about it, during his broadcasts and on a promotional tour in the second half of 1973 (Jack 1995: 228–9).

Following early trade press reviews (e.g. Murphy 1973: 20), the first reviews in the general press accompanied the film's Los Angeles premiere at the beginning of August (see, for example, Canby 1973: D1; Reed 1973: 5; cp. Baxter 1999: 148–9), with another wave coming when it opened in New York on 12 August. On 15 August, the day *American Graffiti* was first shown in cities beyond Los Angeles and New York,[2] *Variety* noted that the film had received 13 'favorable' reviews in New York ('N.Y. Critics' Opinions' 1973: 7), while the *New York Times* reported on 19 August that out of 17 reviews, 15 had been 'favorable' and two 'mixed' ('*American Graffiti*' 1973: D12). Apart from professional critics, regular cinemagoers who had already seen and liked the film were spreading the news. Positive word of mouth had started with the small number of test screenings in Los Angeles and then grew exponentially with the film's commercial release across the country from August onwards.

In this way, despite Universal's comparatively small expenditure on paid-for advertising, people were made aware of the fact that *American Graffiti* was in the cinemas and encouraged to think that it was worth watching, in particular if they had a special interest in its young director and in the changes Hollywood had been undergoing in recent years; if they liked classic rock 'n' roll music and the vocal antics of Wolfman Jack; if they were old enough to be inclined to look back on their teen years or young enough to compare their present teen experience with that of 1962; or if they wanted to get a fresh perspective on contemporary America by immersing themselves in its recent past (especially if, like Lucas told the *New York Times*, they felt that in 1973 America was undergoing important changes, just like it had in the 1960s). As it turned out, from the beginning many such people bought tickets for the film.

American Graffiti premiered on the largest screen of the Avco Cinema Center in Los Angeles on 1 August 1973 and immediately broke house records (possibly because the cinema was less than a mile from the UCLA campus and could count on drawing a large student crowd, including many cinephiles).[3] The film repeated its success when it opened at the Sutton Theatre in New York on 12 August. After two weeks in which it had been shown initially in only one, then two cinemas, the film ran in a steadily increasing number of movie theatres in a selection of cities around the country from 15 August. In many of them, *American Graffiti* played for months; in December *Boxoffice* reported that the film was in its 10th week in St. Louis, its 14th week in St. Paul, its 18th week in Cincinnati, Portland (Oregon) and Seattle, and in its 19th week in Denver, Detroit, Lansing, Minneapolis and San Jose, with no end to the film's run in these cities in sight.

By the end of 1973, *American Graffiti* had earned $10.3 million in rentals and was ranked as the tenth highest-grossing film of the year – tenth out of a total of 219 new films released in the United States in 1973, including 132 releases by the major studios Columbia, MGM, Paramount, Fox, United Artists, Universal and Warner Bros (Finler 1988: 280; Steinberg 1980: 27; 'Big Rental Films of 1973' 1974: 19). *American Graffiti* continued to be shown in the new year and was given a boost by the five Oscar nominations it received – for Best Picture, Best Director, Best Original Screenplay, Best Film Editing and Best Supporting Actress (Candy Clark) –, while being listed by the *New York Times* as one of the ten best films of 1973, and by *Time* as one of the eleven best films of the year. In addition, it won awards for Best Screenplay from the National Society of Film Critics and the New York Film Critics, as well as the Golden Globe for Best Film in the 'Musical/Comedy' category from the Hollywood Foreign Press Association (Steinberg 1980: 174, 178, 248–9, 263, 270, 296).

Publicity for these honours reminded people of the film's existence and assured them of its special quality, thus encouraging them to see it. Indeed, the film's box office performance in 1974 turned out to be extraordinary. In February 1974, *American Graffiti* was reported to have earned $21 million in rentals (Farber 1974/1999: 33), doubling its revenues from 1973, and by the end of that year it was twice as much again with $41.2 million ('Updated All-Time Film Champs' 1975: 26). The film's run continued across the next two years so that by the end of 1975 it had earned $45 million, and by the end of 1976 $47.3 million ('All-Time Film Rental Champs' 1977: 16; 'All-Time Film Rental Champs' 1976: 20). When the film finally disappeared from American movie theatres, it did not stay away for long, because, in the wake of the huge success of Lucas's next feature, *Star Wars, American Graffiti* was re-released in 1978,[4] earning $8.6 million, so as to bring the total up to $55.9 million (Steinberg 1980: 5).

What is most remarkable about *American Graffiti*'s success is its box office performance in 1974. The film earned a huge amount of money – $30.9 million – at a stage in its release (from six to eighteen months after its premiere) when other movies from that period tended to be played out. For example, the top ten of the end-of-year chart for 1973 included four films that were released just before *American Graffiti*: *Deliverance* (Boorman, released in July; earning $18 million in 1973, which is 80% of the total revenues it had earned by the end of 1978); *Live and Let Die* (Hamilton, June, earning 97% of its total during 1973), *Paper Moon* (Bogdanovich, June, 78%) and *Jesus Christ Superstar* (Jewison, June, 79%) (Steinberg 1980: 6–8, 27). By contrast, *American Graffiti* had earned only 20% of its total by the end of 1973, generating 57% the following year.

In addition to the film's exceptional performance in 1974, the enormous size and likely composition of its audience is worth taking a closer look at. Since *American Graffiti*'s box office gross ($115 million) was 2.06 times its rentals ($55.9 million), it is possible to calculate the ticket sales for each year (rentals times 2.06 divided by the average ticket price for that year [Steinberg 1980: 44]): 12 million tickets were sold in 1973, 34 million in 1974, 3.8 million in 1975, 2.3 million in 1976 and 7.6 million in 1978. The total (59.7 million tickets) amounts to around 80% of the size of the baby boom. Even the youngest baby boomers (those born in the mid 1960s) had reached their teenage years by the time *American Graffiti* was re-released in 1978.

Assuming that *American Graffiti* was a film primarily for teenagers and people in their twenties, these figures suggest that the film's audience was largely made up of baby boomers and that, in turn, the majority of baby boomers (perhaps as much as 80%) saw the film at the cinema. This suggestion is compatible with the results of a Motion Picture Association of America (MPAA) survey which found that in 1973 of all tickets sold to cinemagoers over 11 (the assumption being that the number of tickets sold to children under 12 was negligible) in 1973 73% were bought by those in the 12–29 age range, that is those born between 1944 and 1961; by 1975 the share for people in the 12–29 age range (b. 1946–63) had gone up slightly to 74% ('Population Profile Favors Pix' 1975: 3). If around three-quarters of all cinema tickets in 1973/74 were bought by baby boomers, then it is certainly safe to assume that baby boomers bought at least the same percentage, and most probably – given the obvious youth appeal of the film – an even bigger share, of all tickets for *American Graffiti*. In light of the fact that between the early 1960s, when the first baby boomers turned 17 and the early 1970s, the high-school graduation rate was between 70% and 75% (Wattenberg 1976: 379), and that the large majority (75–76%) of high-school dropouts never went to the cinema or only once a year ('Population Profile Favors Pix' 1975: 3), it is very likely that almost all tickets for *American Graffiti* were bought by high-school graduates and current high-school students and that almost all high-school-educated baby boomers bought tickets for the movie.

Critical Reception

When trying to find out what people enjoyed about a movie and how they made sense of it a few decades ago, it is rarely possible to examine statements they made at the time about their experience. The major exceptions are the publications of film reviewers who do not only describe and evaluate the movie in question, but also evoke their own experience of watching it and often comment on the (observed or presumed) responses of regular cinemagoers. Sometimes they step back from their reviewing duties so as to reflect on the impact of a particular movie, which is what Aljean Harmetz did in a *New York Times* article in December 1973 with regards to *American Graffiti*.

The article opens with her answer to the question 'Where were you in '62?': 'I was changing the diapers of my year-old son and watching my abdomen expand with the relentless growth of my second child' (Harmetz 1973: D13). Born in 1929, she was one of the mothers of the last wave of baby boomers. She remembered the film's music only as 'noise' and, partly due to her religious upbringing, 'I cannot even rummage through my memories to find some kinship' with the film's young protagonists: 'I never went to a high school dance or had a hamburger and cherry Coke at the local rendezvous'. 'Why then', she asked, 'does this extremely specific account of adolescents prowling the streets of a small California city [...] move me to such sadness for my lost past?'

She reported that

> [m]ost reviews of the film – many written by men and women who, like the director George Lucas, graduated from high school around 1962 – stress the innocence of that moment in time compared to all

the assassinations and polluted rivers and governmental invasions of privacy that have come after it.

(Harmetz 1973: D13)

As Harmetz pointed out, there was in fact nothing innocent about the United States in the early 1960s: 'The year before *American Graffiti*'s sock hop in the high school gym had brought the Bay of Pigs invasion and a renewed intensification of the Cold War', and 'on that autumn night' in 1962 'there were already Russian missiles in Cuba. The end of the world was always potentially around the corner' (ibid.).[5]

Hence, she argued, '[w]hat makes *American Graffiti* so extraordinary a film is not that it recreates for us the world's innocence but that it recreates our own innocence', by which she meant 'that last moment' in everybody's youthful development 'when choices must be made and keys must be turned in the locks of the future' about whether to stay at home or leave, what career to pursue and who to be with: '*American Graffiti* is a melancholy film, pervaded with a sense that no choice can possibly be the right choice simply because choosing forecloses on the future' (Harmetz 1973: D13). Selecting one path means turning away from all other possible paths, in most cases – and especially with regards to a teenager's grander plans – for good. Harmetz ended her article 'rather wistfully': 'Typing this, I wonder [...] whatever happened to my quite rational decision, made at the age of 15, to spend my life searching for Atlantis?' (ibid.). And she pointed out that the depth of her experience of the film was simply not available to her 12-year-old son, 'a movie connoisseur' who only 'responded with guarded enthusiasm to *American Graffiti*', because, '[f]or him, everything is still possible. He can live a dozen lives in fantasy before choice becomes irrevocable' (ibid.).

Such complex reflections cannot be expected from every piece of journalistic writing on *American Graffiti* in 1973, but cumulatively these pieces do paint a picture of people's responses to the film at that time, at least as far as the educated middle class is concerned, which, as discussed in the previous section, made up the vast majority of the movie's audience (it has to be kept in mind, though, that the reviewers discussed here were mostly born between the 1910s [e.g. Hollis Alpert, b. 1916, and Pauline Kael, b. 1919] and the mid 1940s [e.g. Jay Cocks, b. 1944], thus barely overlapping with the film's main baby boom audience).

While reviewers of *American Graffiti* picked up on the main themes of the film's press book, they went beyond it by placing much more emphasis on George Lucas.[6] It was not just the case that, in conjunction with providing a basic plot summary, some reviewers pointed out that '[t]he story is loosely based on Lucas's memories of his late teens' (Alpert 1973: 41), or that *American Graffiti* 'is a highly personal film, drawn from Lucas's own experience' (Canby 1973: D6);[7] there was also a more general appreciation, even celebration, of his work on this film, which sometimes included comments on his first feature as well. Jay Cocks (1973: 58), for example, described *THX 1138* as 'a cool, cautionary science-fiction tale' which 'established him as a director of great technical range and resources'; now *American Graffiti* 'reveals a new and welcome depth of feeling'. Stephen Farber (1973: D1) proclaimed: 'at 28 [Lucas] is already one of the world's master directors'.

There was considerable disagreement between reviewers about the construction of the film's story. For some, it was all too obvious and simplistic: 'If there is a flaw, it is that the story is put together too neatly. Four threads are developed and then knotted together a bit artificially' (Alpert 1973: 41). By contrast, other reviewers declared that the film was *not* concerned about traditional storytelling at all: 'the picture is rather loose, formless, seems to circle the block endlessly like one of its star cars, and at times gets stuck in neutral' (Sweeney 1973: 14). Indeed, *American Graffiti* 'is a film that just sort of idles along, like a 1960 Chevy [...] cruising down the flat, neon-lit main street of a small California town looking for some action' (ibid.). For these writers, watching the film was akin to cruising.

Quite a few reviewers noted that (classic) cars were at the very heart of *American Graffiti*: 'This flick is the most car-car movie you'll see in a long, long while' ('The Brakes' 1973: 75). The film's focus on moving vehicles – most of the action 'takes place inside, on top, underneath or within spitting distance of cars' – and on the young people driving around in them, 'out of boredom and in their obsession with movement', was seen to express one of its main themes: 'young lives going nowhere in particular but with a debonair manner, a good deal of humor and a lot of decent feelings' (Canby 1973: D1); 'you feel stimulated by the drive through town, and you also feel trapped in the circle; there's no way out', especially not for John Milner who 'knows that his only future is in the car graveyard he haunts' (Farber 1973: D6). Many reviewers agreed that, with the exception of Curt, the young people in *American Graffiti* were shown to be stuck in their home town and its particular way of life, going round in circles rather than moving forward (in addition to the reviews mentioned earlier in this paragraph, also see Cocks 1973: 58; Genauer 1973: 34; Gilliatt 1973: 67; Greenspun 1973: 21; Zimmerman 1973: 93). Yet, with few exceptions (notably Kissel 1973: 18), they did not think that the film was looking down on its protagonists, its historical period and its small-town setting. Rather, *American Graffiti* vividly brought all this to life, aiming to offer a wholly immersive experience to viewers.

Music was seen to be central to the experience of the film. Many reviewers praised the selection of songs from the late 1950s and early 1960s: 'a splendid choice of time-drenched music' (Winsten 1973: 21), including some of 'the most rock 'n' roll popular hits of the time' (Murray 1973: D5). They noted that '[t]he sound track of *American Graffiti* is deliberately obtrusive', not so much subtly supporting the story being told than overtly shaping the audience's engagement with that story: 'It sets the period, establishes the mood, raucously accompanies the action' (Alpert 1973: 41). Indeed, it puts the audience in the same position as the people listening to that music in the world of the story: 'by keeping it in the background of almost every scene, Lucas mesmerizes us right along with the characters' (Farber 1973: D1). The music served both to indicate the pastness of the action and to erase any sense of historical distance and detachment from it.

Reviewers related *American Graffiti* to previous films for and about teenagers: '[Candy Clarke] could easily be mistaken in real life, as she admits that she is in the film, for Sandra Dee' (Alpert 1973: 41). In addition to major studio releases such as Sandra Dee movies and *Rebel Without a Cause* (referenced in Kael [1973: 154], who also mentions MGM's Mickey Rooney vehicles of the 1930s and 1940s), reviewers linked *American Graffiti* to low-budget exploitation pictures made and released by independents. According to A.D. Murphy, the film occupied the 'very lonely ground between the uptight misunderstood teenage mellers' of the 1950s and early 1960s and 'the beach-party fluff on which American International held the only successful patents' in the same period (1973: 20).

Like the film's soundtrack, its generic affiliation served to transport spectators back to their own youth or, in the case of younger viewers, to their country's popular-cultural past. There was some disagreement about how productively *American Graffiti* engaged with its generic predecessors. For Pauline Kael (1973: 154) the film 'isn't much more than an update', filled with overly familiar 'stock characters'. In her view, the movie neither transcended the limitations of the teen film nor did it aim seriously to engage its audience, which it merely 'invites to share in a fond, jokey view of its own adolescence'. By contrast, Jay Cocks (1973: 58) argued that 'Lucas mocks, carefully and compassionately, the conventions and stereotypes of a genre as well as a generation' with a view of creating a sense of 'lingering melancholy', because his film shows its characters, with the exception of Curt, to be 'locked in – to careers, to whole lives', and also, he implied, to the conventions of the teen genre. Thus, in this critic's view, *American Graffiti* 'compassionately' revealed the shortcomings of the teen film genre as well as of the decade and the way of life it was so closely associated with.

The majority of reviewers shared Cocks's positive view of the film's qualities and achievements, even when comparing it to more recent releases dealing with the experiences of young people and with the past. The writers who referenced some of the key films of this cycle – *The Last Picture Show, Summer of '42* and its sequel *Class of '44* (Bogart, 1973) – tended to highlight the superior quality of *American Graffiti* (Alpert 1973: 41; Farber 1973: D1; Greenspun 1973: D21; Murphy 1973: 20; Sweeney 1973: 14). According to Farber, '[t]he nostalgia boom has finally produced a lasting work of art' comparable to recent masterpieces of American cinema such as *Bonnie and Clyde* and *Five Easy Pieces* (Rafelson, 1970).

Many reviewers used the words 'nostalgia' or 'nostalgic' to characterise *American Graffiti*, often relating the film, as the critics just cited did, to a recent cycle of nostalgic movies or to a broader nostalgic trend in American culture of the early 1970s, with the Broadway run of *Grease* being mentioned as another important manifestation of this trend (Cocks 1973: 58). While some critics wrote about nostalgia for the 1950s (e.g. Cocks 1973: 58) or for '[t]he 50s (which lasted until about 1965)' (Kissel 1973: 18), others referred to '1960s nostalgia' (Canby 1973: 1). One writer wondered: 'I would have thought that the time was ripe for more filmic and fictional re-creation of the Fifties, and thus I was somewhat unprepared for a nostalgic treatment of 1962. Was it all that long ago?' (Alpert 1973: 41). His answer was: 'If you're thirty, ten years is a third of a lifetime, and those dear, dead days have a pleasant glow about them'.

The 'pleasant glow' of nostalgic feelings was considered a potential problem because it could lead to distorted perceptions of the past and might invite an escape from the present ('lovers of 1962 will only pass reluctantly through those theatre doors back to the realities of 1973' [Murray 1973: D5]). Yet, with few exceptions (such as Kael 1973: 154), critics argued that Lucas and his collaborators had successfully tackled this problem: 'nostalgia [...] never corrupts the discipline of the film or cheapens the sorrows of its characters' (Canby 1973: 1); '[t]he characters whom Lucas creates are [...] seen with a sense of humor and distance which rescues them from seeming to be figures of easy nostalgia' (Gilliatt 1973: 67). And while *American Graffiti* 'keeps you hip-deep in memory and reminiscence', one critic argued, 'the sense of real people's history becomes stronger' at the very end of the film through the postscript (Winsten 1973: 21).

Underpinning most reviews was the idea that the filmic recreation of life in the recent past, of a particular time and place, could provide a valuable and enjoyable experience. This might involve a generalised and abstracted sense of being able to connect ('[g]reat films absorb the audience in a distinctive world' [Farber 1973: 1]) or reconnect: 'If you're nostalgic [...] this should take you home again' (Chis 1973: 60). Or it could refer to something more specific: 'It's always nice to remember pleasant times and the era that this film so effectively captures is perhaps the last age of exuberant optimism American adolescents will ever enjoy' (Murray 1973: D5), 'an age of sublime innocence' (Carroll 1973: 45). Critics disagreed about whether *American Graffiti* delivered an accurate and convincing recreation of past times. Several critics (none more so than Pauline Kael [1973: 154]) thought that the film failed to do this, because it adhered to clichéd conceptions of the past, and to the conventions of the cultural forms associated with it, rather than capturing its reality: 'I refuse to believe that this is what kids were like in '62' (Genauer 1973: 34). Most reviewers, however, were positive: '[the film] qualifies as a veritable masterpiece, an uncannily excellent re-creation of the teenage scene just 10 or so years ago' (Murray 1973: D5); 'no sociological treatise could duplicate the movie's success in remembering exactly how it was to be alive at that cultural instant' (Ebert 1973).

Across the majority of reviews, there is a strong sense that the period recreated in the film was full of tensions, as was the life of the teenagers it featured. There were dissenting views, as when Hollis Alpert declared that '[t]he worries of the kids are not great [...] and all problems are pretty much resolved by morning' (1973: 41). Other critics similarly felt that the film was trivialising American teenage life in the early 1960s (Kael 1973: 154; Kissel 1973: 18; Frank 1973: 15). Yet, contrary to Aljean Harmetz's claim (discussed at the beginning of this section), the word 'innocence' was rarely used to characterise the historical period the film was dealing with or the way the film was portraying it, or indeed the youth of its characters. Howard Kissel (1973: 18) directly challenged the idea that 'the 50s' (which he extended into the early 1960s) were 'a period of great innocence': 'those years were not as sunlit as we seem to remember. [...] [We] forget air raid drills and I.D. bracelets. [...] It was, in fact, a decade initiated by Sen. Joseph McCarthy'. He did not argue that *American Graffiti* offered an idealised version of this historical period; instead he judged the film to be an ineffective 'satire' of 'the 50s'.

While Kathleen Carroll (1973: 45) referred to the film's historical period as 'an age of sublime innocence', she nevertheless acknowledged that the teenagers in the film were at a crucial point in their lives, 'when their future hangs in the balance' – the times may have been 'innocent' but there was nothing innocent about the decisions young people had to make. And when Stephen Farber (1973: 1) wrote that *American Graffiti* is set 'at the tail end of an era' and 'freezes the last moment of American innocence', he emphasised that its young protagonists 'do have an intuitive sense that their culture is disintegrating', the film thus registering 'how radically the country will be shaken and polarized by the cataclysms of the next few years'. Whatever 'innocence' there may once have been, the film acknowledged that it always already contained the seeds of its own destruction. What is more, Farber argued that while the film 'retrieves the exuberance of a carefree moment of youth [...] by the end it is suffused with a feeling of lost opportunities, shattered possibilities' (6).

In this and other ways, the majority of critics pointed out that the film took the characters and their problems very seriously, acknowledging that much was at stake in the decisions they had to make and that they lived in a society and at a time that was marked by conflict and social change. Jay Cocks (1973: 58), for example, wrote:

> This superb and singular film catches not only the charm and tribal energy of the teen-age 1950s but also the listlessness and the resignation that underscored it all. [...] Few films have shown quite so well the eagerness, the sadness, the ambitions and small defeats of a generation of young Americans.

Some critics went beyond identifying 'a generation of young Americans' as the focus of *American Graffiti* by including themselves in that generation (although they tended to be a few years older); the film thus was about 'us'. Hence Roger Ebert (b. 1942) began his review with recollections about his first car and his cruising days in the 1950s, before noting that watching the film made him see 'how unprepared we were for [...] the series of hammer blows beginning with the assassination of President Kennedy' (Ebert 1973). Rex Reed (b. 1938) wrote: 'This is the story of all our lives', and 'an absolute must for anyone who has as much nostalgia about growing up in the late 1950s and early 1960s as I do' (1973: 5). He pointed out that his nostalgia was a complicated and 'highly-charged emotional experience': 'It's a period I look back on with intense pain and sadness'.

Several reviewers stated that for them (as for Aljean Harmetz) the film was not so much about a specific historical period, but, more generally, about a particular stage in everyone's life. In this context, it is worth quoting the opening and conclusion of Paul Zimmermann's (1973: 93) thoughtful review at some length:

> In our last years of high school, we thought we were making choices that would shape the rest of our lives. Only later did we realize that many of those choices had already been made for us by our genes and social programming. At 28, director George Lucas is young enough to recall and re-create that heady, scary period of self-definition. But he's also old enough to understand how illusory that sense of infinite possibility really was. This dual awareness gives his brilliant, bittersweet memoir [...] its tension and tough-minded complexity. [...] Lucas has captured a moment recognizable to every generation, when all of us are shoring up our sapling egos with the roles and defenses we would need in the years ahead.

Pauline Kael (1973: 154) refused to be included in any collective projected by the film, because, she argued, this collective was not inclusive. In her view, the film was about and for 'white middle-class boys': 'Not for women, not for blacks or Orientals or Puerto Ricans, not for homosexuals, not for the poor'. Yet, as noted above, Aljean Harmetz did not feel excluded (if she felt far removed from the film's protagonists, it was because of her age and her strict upbringing, not because of her gender), nor did Kathleen Carroll (1973: 45), who concluded her review: '[*American Graffiti*] is a richly entertaining movie guaranteed to please nearly everyone'.

In a long article surveying American cinema of 1973, Molly Haskell judged *American Graffiti* to be one of the very few recent releases giving women prominent and strong roles, describing its three female leads as 'spunky girls, fighting with an arsenal of words, gestures, expressions, blackmail [...] and resisting, with all their native resources, the notion of female inferiority' (Haskell 1973: 821). To some extent, Kael (1973: 154) seemed to agree with this by noting that Carol is 'the most entertaining character', and '[b]ecause of the energy of the performers, Laurie and Carol stay in the memory more vividly than the boys'. Her feminist critique of *American Graffiti* was largely based on the absence of the central female characters from the postscript. Finally, the African American critic James Murray did not comment on the whiteness of the film's milieu and highlighted its general appeal: 'Even for those who were not growing up in 1962 or for those parents of 1962 teenagers, this film is a captivating piece of entertainment' (Murray 1973: D5).

The reviewers discussed in this section are not representative of the American population at the time, but their writing does indicate key ways of engaging with, and making sense of, the film, which are likely to have underpinned the responses of the educated baby boomers making up the vast majority of the film's audience. Judging by the reviews, then, *American Graffiti* offered viewers the opportunity to immerse themselves in the past, a past characterised by excitement and fun and a considerable degree of personal freedom, by the necessity to make difficult, potentially life-changing decisions and by severe limitations for teenagers' decision-making: the place they grow up in and the people they grow up with do not just provide a home but are also a kind of trap from which it is difficult to escape. More fundamentally, the film acknowledges, as Harmetz put it, that a decision *for* something is always a decision *against* all the alternatives. So both older and younger baby boomers watching *American Graffiti* probably were, like most of the critics, left with a complex mixture of thoughts and feelings about their adolescence.

The reviews indicate that engaging with *American Graffiti* involved thoughts about how American society had changed. In conjunction with the advertising and publicity surrounding its release, the film (not least its epilogue) created the impression that, for better and for worse, since the 1950s and early 1960s certain forms of social unity and homogeneity had given way to division and diversity, optimism and naivety to pessimism and realism, continuity and stasis to discontinuity and transformation, and political disengagement to political mobilisation. *American Graffiti* implied that one of the key drivers of such societal change was the baby boom generation itself.

Baby Boomers and American Culture

American Graffiti was made by, about and for baby boomers. By 1973, early baby boomers were in their 20s, most having settled down into careers and marriages. They were in a position to look back on the crucial decisions they had made to get to where they were in their individual lives. At the same time, across the 1970s both early and later baby boomers became increasingly concerned about the current state, and the future, of American politics, the economy and the environment (as discussed in the Introduction) which gave them a collective reason for revisiting the past. By doing so, they might, among other things, be able to find a new perspective on the present state of national (and international) affairs, perhaps identifying some of the historical roots of contemporary problems, such an approach certainly being suggested in some of the film's reviews.

What is there to say specifically about younger baby boomers, born between the mid 1950s and the mid 1960s? Arguably, the most important point to make is that there were many more of them than there were older boomers. Before examining this increase, it is necessary to go back to the very definition of the baby boom. The most commonly chosen start date for the baby boom is 1946 because in that year the number of births in the United States was 3.4 million, a 17% increase from the 2.9 million births in 1945 (Colby and Ortman 2014: 3). However, by the standard of the 1930s, 2.9 million was already a high number. During the earlier decade, around 2.5 million babies had been born per year, whereas from 1942 to 1945 the number fluctuated around the 3 million mark (a 20% increase from 1930s figures). So, after the relatively small number of 1930s children becoming teenagers before the mid 1950s, from then on a dramatically increased number of children turned 13 every year.

These unusually large numbers contributed, in conjunction with a range of other factors (e.g. increased prosperity, permissive childrearing and extended schooling, as discussed in the Introduction), to the central place that teenagers and teen culture occupied in American society at that time. A lot has been written about teen culture (especially teen films and pop music) and public concern about teenagers in the 1950s, and about the aging of the early baby boomers, including their involvement in the social movements of the 1960s and their turn to nostalgia in the 1970s, and I have summarised some of this literature in the Introduction.[8] Much less attention has been paid to the fact that the number of annual births in the United States *continued* growing for most of the 1950s (from 3.8 million in 1952 to 4.3 million in the peak year of 1957, a 13% increase), and then only slowly declined (to just over 4 million in 1964; afterwards the figure did not fall below 3.5 million until 1972). This means that the number of baby boomers reaching their teen years in the period 1970–74 was considerably larger than that for the years 1955–59.

It could be expected that in the first half of the 1970s the largest-ever cohort of teenagers was, just as it had been in the second half of the 1950s, considered to be an important topic of public debate as well as a ready-made market for all kinds of products, including popular culture, with many cultural products featuring teens. But the evidence is somewhat mixed. For example, in the late 1960s and early 1970s, Hollywood hit movies were addressed primarily to teenagers and young adults, but they rarely had teenage protagonists. As discussed in Chapter 1, this was changing in 1971 with the release of *Summer of '42, The Last Picture Show* and *A Clockwork Orange*, all three films having successful runs the following year, as did the reissue of *The Graduate* which like *Love Story* (the biggest hit of 1970/71), featured characters at the end or just out of their teens when the story begins.

While all the above films were mainly focused on young male pro-tagonists, from 1972/73 onwards there were several hits featuring young females without equally young male partners. These included *Last Tango in Paris* (Bertolucci, released in January 1973) which was ranked sixth in the end-of-year chart with rentals of $12.6 ('Big Rental Films of 1973' 1974: 19) and co-starred Maria Schneider (b. 1952). There also was the precocious pre-teen starring in the Depression-era comedy *Paper Moon*, released in June 1972 and having a long run into 1973 (with rentals of $13 million by the end of that year ['Updated All-Time Film Champs' 1974: 23]); she was played by Tatum O'Neal (b. 1963). And then, overlapping with the release of *American Graffiti*, came *The Exorcist* (Friedkin), which featured a girl on the cusp of ad-olescence (played by Linda Blair, b. 1959); released in December 1973, by the end of 1974 the film had earned $66.3 million in rentals ('Up-dated All-Time Film Champs' 1975: 26). At this point, *The Exorcist* was ranked fifth in *Variety*'s list of all-time rentals champions, with *Love Story* (shown, as noted earlier, on television in October 1972 with a record-breaking 42.3 rating) and *The Graduate* (shown on television with a 30.5 rating on 8 November 1973 [Steinberg 1980: 33]) following in sixth and seventh place, and *American Graffiti* at number 14.[9]

Films about teens, and those just a little bit younger or older,[10] were certainly becoming very successful in the early 1970s, and it is there-fore possible to say that *American Graffiti* fit an existing hit pattern,[11] especially when considering the overwhelming, ongoing popularity of *The Graduate* and *Love Story* and the fact that *American Graffiti* has a special connection to these two films insofar as together they map out the development of the earliest baby boomers, born in the mid 1940s, from high school to university and into working life.

However, as discussed above, reviews of *American Graffiti* did not so much reference the recent cycle of hit movies about teenagers (and those slightly younger or older), but instead related the film to teen movies of the 1950s and early 1960s, as well as to what critics tended to call 'nostalgia films'. Of course, *Summer of '42*, *The Last Picture Show* and *Class of '44* dealt both with the fairly recent past and with teenag-ers (and *Paper Moon* with a pre-teen and the past). And since 1967 box office charts had been full of movies about American history from the 1920s onwards, most of which lovingly recreated the past or used it to offer a new perspective on the present or, like *American Graffiti*, did both. The years from 1972 to 1974 were the high point of this trend, with long runs for *The Godfather* (set in the late 1940s and early 1950s) and the depression-era comedy *The Sting* (Hill, released in December 1973); by the end of 1974, these films took first and fourth place (with rentals of $85.7 million and $68.5 million, respectively) in *Variety*'s list of all-time box office champions ('Updated All-Time Film Champs' 1975: 26).

American Graffiti thus fit *two* important hit patterns of the first half of the 1970s: films about teenagers (and those a little bit younger or older), and films set in the American past from the 1920s onwards, whereby many of the hits in the former category also belonged, like *American Graffiti*, to the latter. At the same time, *American Graffiti* distinguished itself from the majority of big hits in these two categories by largely avoiding explicit sex, graphic violence, sacrilege and other material known to put off many people (while being particularly appealing to others). Indeed, with the initially 'X'-rated *A Clockwork Orange* continuing its run into 1972 and 1973, the arrival of 'porno chic' in movie theatres in the summer of 1972 (producing massive hits with the hardcore features *Deep Throat* [Damiano, released in June 1972] and *The Devil in Miss Jones* [Damiano, March 1973]), the success of the 'X'-rated *Last Tango in Paris*, and the extraordinarily intense mixture of body horror, violence, sexuality and sacrilege in *The Exorcist*, *American Graffiti* was able to offer a counterpoint to what, for a moment, appeared to be a wide-ranging takeover of mainstream American cinema by what had long been taboo.[12]

Among other things, this was indicated by the film's 'PG' rating, which contrasted with the 'X's and 'R's for so many of the other hit movies that were intended to prevent or discourage anyone under 17 from attending. Intriguingly, on *American Graffiti*'s poster and at the very conclusion of the trailer a note about the film's rating stated: 'PARENTAL GUIDANCE SUGGESTED – SOME MATERIAL MAY NOT BE SUITABLE FOR PRE-TEENAGERS'. This note may well have made the film *more* appealing to young teenagers and to pre-teens who were able to purchase tickets without any restrictions at the box office ('PG' simply signalled that children should consult their parents about it).

The film's rating and its avoidance of taboo material are of particular importance when thinking about its appeal to women. Surveys across the late 1960s and the 1970s revealed that female respondents objected particularly strongly to sex and violence in the movies and to 'X'-rated films, while their preferred types of film included love stories and comedies (Krämer 2005: 60–2). With its, by the standards of the time, as noted by Molly Haskell (1973: 821), unusual foregrounding of female characters, its focus on comedy and on romantic relationships of various kinds, *American Graffiti* had a lot to offer to female cinemagoers. Indeed, a survey of female high-school students found that *American Graffiti* was their second favourite movie of the year, closely behind the (nostalgic) romantic drama *The Way We Were* (Pollack, 1973) ('The Class of 1974' 1974: 57).[13]

All of this helps to understand why *American Graffiti* became a box office success, but it does not yet explain the film's exceptional performance during 1974. Here a more detailed look at television can provide some pointers. First of all, one can note that teenagers (and those slightly younger or older) were prominent characters in top-rated television shows in the early 1970s, reflecting the growth in the number of teenagers in American society during this period. The biggest ratings hits of these years included the sitcom *All in the Family* (CBS, 1971–79, the top-rated show of the 1971/72 season as well as the next four seasons) and the depression-era drama *The Waltons* (CBS, 1972–81, at number 19 in 1972/73, number 2 in 1973/74 and number 8 in 1974/75). Both shows revolved around families with prominent roles for teenagers and young adults: John Boy, the central character of *The Waltons*, is 17 years old at the beginning of the series; in *All in the Family* lead character Archie Bunker's daughter Gloria and her husband Michael are slightly older.

Most importantly, echoing the family focus of both shows, and inhabiting the historical middle-ground between the 1930s setting of *The Waltons* and the contemporary setting of *All in the Family*, there was the sitcom *Happy Days*, set in the late 1950s and focusing on teenagers and their parents.[14] So far I have only mentioned this series, as most writers on the subject do, as a cultural phenomenon that was helped along by the success of *American Graffiti* (see, for example, Staiger 2000: 114–9), but the reverse argument also applies. The story of Midwestern high-school student Richie Cunningham, his family and his friends was first presented in a segment of the ABC anthology series *Love, American Style* in February 1972 (Marshall 2005: 80–1; Staiger 2000: 115). Ron Howard's performance as Richie appears to have influenced Lucas's decision to cast him in *American Graffiti*, and the casting of Howard in this movie and its later success in turn encouraged ABC to take another look at the anthology episode, which had originally been intended as a series pilot, and to commission *Happy Days* (Marshall 2005: 82).

Happy Days premiered on 15 January 1974 and ran until 7 May 1974, becoming the 16th highest-rated TV show of the 1973/74 season with an average rating of 21.5,[15] which means that more than a fifth of all American households had tuned into this sitcom every single week for almost four months. Not only was *Happy Days* set in the late 1950s (close to *American Graffiti*'s 1962 which, as previously noted, was widely understood in terms of an enlarged concept of 'the fifties') and not only did it have a small-town rather than a big-city feel (although Milwaukee certainly was much larger than Modesto), but it also played 'Rock Around the Clock' in its opening credit sequence, starred Ron Howard as a teenager and featured an older rock 'n' roller (Arthur Fonzarelli, known as 'Fonzie' or 'the Fonz' and echoing *American Graffiti*'s John Milner). In other words, for the first few months of 1974, *Happy Days* served as an extended trailer for *American Graffiti*. This (together with the continuing huge success in 1974 of the soundtrack album) helps to explain why *American Graffiti* was so unusually successful in 1974. And although *Happy Days* lost a lot of its audience during its second season from September 1974 to May 1975 (Staiger 2000: 122), it continued to serve as a constant reminder to millions of people that the actor playing Richie Cunningham appeared in a closely related movie still playing in cinemas. This continued in the 1975/76 season when *Happy Days* was at number 11 in the annual chart with a 21.3 rating and in 1976/77 when it was at number 1 with an extraordinary 31.5 rating, which was only slightly reduced to 31.4 in 1977/78 when it came in at number 2.

While *Happy Days* reached all audience segments (with a, for television, typical bias towards women), it was unusually popular with teenagers (as well as younger children), especially after more emphasis was placed on Fonzie and his friendship with Richie Cunningham in the third season (Staiger 2000: 119–39). For older viewers (among them many baby boomers born in the 1940s and the first half of the 1950s), enjoyment of the show must have had a lot to do with a nostalgic revisiting of their own youth and their country's past. But what about teenage viewers? Perhaps the results of a 1976 Australian audience study (summarised in Noble 1983: 109–11) can be applied to American viewers: 'adolescents overwhelmingly reported that they had learnt a great range of social behaviours from *Happy Days*', most notably 'how to be "cool"', 'how to relate to the opposite sex and to friends' as well as parents and 'how to be themselves' (110). There were some differences in the responses of males and females, indicating that 'what the adolescents said they had learnt was appropriate to their sex roles', yet 'in areas such as relating to parents [...] and learning to be themselves [...], there were no significant differences between the sexes, notwithstanding the male dominance of the casting in *Happy Days*' (111).

These results indicate how American teenage viewers of *Happy Days* may have engaged with what they saw on the screen. Among many other things, they 'learn familiarity with various situations simply by watching other people cope with such situations' and use their viewing experience 'for anticipatory socialisations into roles which they envisaged they would have to enact in the future' (111). Such 'anticipatory' uses may also have been at work in teenagers' engagement with *American Graffiti*, with regards to both current challenges in their lives (to do with romance, friendship and decisions about the future) and longer-term developments. In the same way that the film looks back, nostalgically and critically, from 1973 to 1962, teenage viewers could imagine how they might see their present lives from the point of view of the people they would become in the following decade.

In addition to *Happy Days*, there were further, more or less teen-focused ratings hits that were closely connected to *American Graffiti*. The *Happy Days* spin-off *Laverne & Shirley*, co-starring *American Graffiti*'s Cindy Williams as one of two young working women in late 1950s Milwaukee, was first shown in January 1976 and immediately became one of the most successful shows (at number 3 for the 1975/76 season with a 27.5 rating), moving to second place the following season (with a 30.9 rating) and then to the top spot (31.6) (cp. Staiger 2000: 112–3, 131–40). What is more, *American Graffiti*'s Mackenzie Phillips, now a fully-fledged teenager, had her own hit show, *One Day at a Time* (CBS, 1975–84), from December 1975 onwards; during its first three seasons, it was ranked 12th, 8th and 10th with ratings of around 23.[16] Thus the tens of millions of people following *Happy Days*, *Laverne & Shirley* and *One Day at a Time* were, more or less directly, reminded on a weekly basis that it might be worth watching the movie that their stars were appearing in, which helps to explain why *American Graffiti* continued to be so successful at the box office after 1974.

Conclusion

Even before its official release in August 1973, *American Graffiti* had been gaining some momentum with critics and cinemagoers, especially young cinephiles and music fans, during test and press screenings (as discussed in Chapter 1). This momentum continued to build during the film's slow roll-out in the autumn and into the new year, bolstered by positive word of mouth, excellent reviews, extensive publicity for George Lucas and his movie, Wolfman Jack's promotional activities and the release of a soundtrack album, the film's considerable success during the awards season and the initial TV run of *Happy Days* from

January 1974 onwards. In addition, *American Graffiti* profited from the fact that it fit two prominent box office hit patterns of the years 1971–74 – films about teenagers (and those just a little bit younger or older) and films about the fairly recent American past – while at the same time avoiding the transgressive material that characterised so many of the hit movies of these years, thus offering a kind of cinematic counterprogramming.

American Graffiti was initially promoted and received (by reviewers) as a semi-autobiographical film by an unusually young filmmaker, and as an immersive and emotionally engaging experience, vividly bringing to the screen a compelling vision of adolescence and of the recent past, while dealing complexly with difficult developments both in individual lives and in the country as a whole. *American Graffiti* was widely understood as being linked to teen films of the 1950s and 1960s, and to the recent cycle of nostalgic films about teenagers, and judged to be superior to its predecessors.

Several reviewers referred to the late 1960s and early 1970s as a period of rapid and particularly disruptive change although hardly any of them explicitly mentioned specific events or developments. Perhaps they felt that readers would know what they were talking about – everything from assassinations and protests to environmental damage, stagflation and the Vietnam War. Reviewers tended to agree that, compared to the present, the 1950s and early 1960s had been a simpler, even 'innocent' time, and yet it was also perceived as a time of change. Most critics did not understand *American Graffiti* as an invitation, or an opportunity, to escape from present-day reality, but as an effective means for gaining a fresh perspective on it from an in places uncomfortable confrontation with the personal and national past, and with important decisions that had had to be made.

Both the publicity for the film and its reviews characterised it as the portrait of a generation, referring, in the first instance, to those born in the 1940s, but also, implicitly, including those who had entered their teen years since the early 1960s. The almost 60 million tickets sold for *American Graffiti* during its long run until 1976 and its re-release in 1978 matched the number of baby boomers who had completed, or were going to, high school. Like the film's reviewers, older baby boomers, mostly settled into marriages and careers, appeared to be using *American Graffiti* to reflect, by no means uncritically, on their country's past and on their own teenage years and, indirectly, on their present situation as well. Younger baby boomers were able, through *American Graffiti*, to learn more about, and to reflect on, their present stage in life, examining it as if from a future point of view, while learning about their country's past.

Older baby boomers settling into adult life; younger baby boomers coping with adolescence; teenagers (and those a little bit younger or older) being featured in hit movies and TV shows; hit movies and shows set in the recent past – the high point of these converging trends was the success of *Happy Days* and *Laverne & Shirley*, *Grease* and *Animal House* in 1977 and 1978 (Krämer 2020: 145–63), by which time even the youngest baby boomers had entered their teen years. The enormous impact of Lucas's follow-up to *American Graffiti*, *Star Wars*, was arguably a consequence of this convergence, because of its teenage protagonists, its evocation of entertainment forms of the past (movie serials from the 1930s and 40s shown on television in the 1950s) and its story being set in the past as well, albeit not the recent past (as per the first part of the movie's tagline 'A long time ago in a galaxy far, far away...').

Thus, in the 1970s, the individual experience of life-stages as well as collective cultural and socio-political experiences shaped the viewing preferences of baby boomers, comprising both teenagers and those having recently entered adulthood, so as to give rise to the success of nostalgia and teen protagonists in the movies and on TV. This success prepared the ground for, and then sustained, the astonishing box office performance of *American Graffiti*, which in turn helped the success of certain TV shows and provided a model for future hit movies, among them George Lucas's next project. For much of the decade, hugely successful hit movies and TV shows combining teen protagonists and nostalgia allowed the baby boom generation to watch, celebrate and question itself and the country it lived in.

Notes

1 For more interviews with Lucas in 1973/74 see 'Young Directors, New Films' (1973: 45–6), Sturhahn (1974/1999: 14–32) and Farber (1974/1999: 33–44).

2 Key cities are listed in the advertisement for *American Graffiti* printed in *Variety*, 1 August 1973, p. 15.

3 This information is taken from an ad Universal placed in *Variety* on 13 August 1973 (p. 11). The rest of this paragraph is based on this ad as well as two others: *Variety*, 1 August 1973, p. 15; and *Boxoffice*, 10 December 1973, p. 5.

4 As *American Graffiti* was re-released in May 1978 (https://www.imdb.com/title/tt0069704/releaseinfo?ref_=tt_dt_dt), it is possible that Universal was trying to cash in on the much anticipated release of the film adaptation of the long-running Broadway hit *Grease* in June 1978.

5 Harmetz was by no means alone in pointing to the darker side of the earlier period; cp. Marcus (2004: 15–22).

6 For previous discussions of the film's reviews, see Staiger (2000: 117), Baxter (1999: 148–50), Jenkins (1998: 49–50) and Pollock (1990: 122–3).

7 Somewhat predictably the review in Lucas's home town paper pointed out many local references and highlighted the fact that 'director George Lucas, 29, spent his gee-whiz adolescence' in Modesto; less predictably, the reviewer was not very impressed with the film, suggesting that the actors 'probably will not be remembered' and declaring that '[t]he music sounded monotonous' (Herman 1973).

8 In addition to the literature cited in the Introduction, see Petigny (2009: 179–223), Nash (2006: 168–214), Medovoi (2005), Palladino (1996: 97–188), Breines (1992) and Gilbert (1986) on teenagers and the 1950s. James (2017: 23–91), Brode (2015: 1–135), Klein (2011: 100–37), Tropiano (2006: 17–85), Doherty (1988) as well as McGee and Robertson (1982: 18–96) focus on the teen-oriented films of this decade, while Hall (2014: 1–68) and Altschuler (2003: 3–160) focus on teen-oriented music. Dennis (2008: 1–102) discusses teenagers in films, on television and in pop music of the 1950s and early 1960s.

9 In addition, broadcasts of *The Wizard of Oz* (Fleming, 1939), starring a teenage Judy Garland, achieved high ratings not only in the 1950s and 1960s, but also in the early to mid 1970s, as did *West Side Story* and various made-for-TV Waltons movies, teen dramas and teen comedies (Steinberg 1980: 32–6).

10 Note that *American Graffiti*'s ensemble cast features both a key character who is no longer a teenager (John Milner) and one who is barely old enough to count as one (Carol).

11 This pattern continued with *The Other Side of the Mountain* (Peerce, 1975), *Tommy* (Russell, 1975), *The Bad News Bears* (Ritchie, 1976), *Star Wars*, *Animal House* and *Grease*; cp. Krämer (2005: 109, 116).

12 Cp. the annual charts in Krämer (2005: 108–9). On 'porno chic' see Cook (2000: 275–6).

13 In this context, it is worth remembering that Candy Clark received an Oscar nomination for Best Supporting Actress. In Quigley's annual poll of film exhibitors, she was identified as one of the ten movie performers 'most likely to achieve major stardom' in the future (Steinberg 1980: 62, 65). For Clark's own retrospective comments on *American Graffiti*, see Rowlands (2012).

14 There is also the success, from 1972 onwards, of *M*A*S*H* (CBS, 1972–83), a sitcom about young army doctors based on the 1970 hit movie, which was set during the early 1950s but was often perceived to have more of a late 1960s feel.

15 See Staiger (2000: 119–20) and https://en.wikipedia.org/wiki/Happy_Days #Episodes.

16 For more on Phillips's life and career, see Phillips (2009).

Coda

American Graffiti was conceived, designed and understood as, among other things, an exploration of the centrality of cars in postwar American culture and of everything that cars stood for. In addition to general prosperity and the fluidity, glamour, competitiveness and adventurousness of youth, the cars in *American Graffiti* represented, in the words of A.D. Murphy's *Variety* review, 'the accumulated junk and materialism of the Eisenhower years, an endowment of tin theology and synthetic values' (1973: 20).

Seen from this perspective, the story of *American Graffiti* revolves around an excessive (emotional as well as material) investment in cars; their status as prestige objects (both for individuals and for communities) rather than as functional devices serving to get people from here to there (instead, in *American Graffiti*, they mostly go round in circles or head towards a crash); the often lethal threat they pose to drivers and others; and the incredible wastefulness of their use (burning fuel all night long). Thus, cars could be said to exemplify much of what many regarded as being wrong with postwar American society – while others, of course, saw them as emblems of technological progress, economic success and personal freedom. *American Graffiti* resonated so strongly with its audience because it celebrated the excesses of consumption associated with fifties and early sixties youth and car culture, and at the same time showed, especially through Curt's storyline, that it was possible, perhaps even necessary, to turn away from these excesses.

Such an understanding of the film was strongly encouraged by the so-called 'oil crisis', or 'energy crisis', which ran parallel to the making and release of *American Graffiti*, climaxing in the autumn of 1973 and the winter of 1973/74, when the film was most widely shown around the country. Ever since the United States had started to import oil in the late 1960s, there had been concerns about the country's dependence on foreign

DOI: 10.4324/9781315545509-5

suppliers for one of the key resources underpinning its energy-intensive economy and car-oriented way of life.[1] These concerns increased considerably in the early 1970s due to occasional oil shortages. They then moved to the very centre of media reporting and public concerns (Neumann 1990: 168) when, during the Arab-Israeli war of October 1973, the Organization of the Petroleum Exporting Countries (OPEC), which was dominated by Arab states, started to boycott the USA and other countries that supported Israel. This boycott lasted until March 1974.

The oil price rose dramatically during this period, and there were worries in the United States about insufficient supplies of heating oil for the winter months and of petrol for cars. At the municipal, state and federal level, governments took all kinds of measures to reduce energy consumption, and strict rationing was being considered, but not implemented, for the population as a whole. There were official pleas, including from the president, to reduce car use and energy consumption, and stricter speed limits were introduced. Many petrol stations had to close for lack of fuel to sell, and long queues formed at those that remained open. Car sales slumped, with the share of smaller cars, especially foreign ones, going up. All of this added a particular poignancy to Milner's comments, in *American Graffiti*, about the glory of wasting fuel, to the many scenes showing small-town streets and parking lots jam-packed with cars, to Terry's declaration of love for Steve's car, to Curt's small, foreign car, etc.[2]

Media reporting about the oil crisis intensified and peaked late in 1973, while surveys found that in January 1974 Americans regarded the oil shortage to be the most important of all problems the country faced (Smith 1985: 273). By the middle of 1974, both media attention to, and public concern about, the country's oil supply had gone down to pre-boycott levels – only to flare up again later that year (Neumann 1990: 168). The oil price had largely stabilised by then, albeit at a much higher level than it had ever been before. Car use and energy consumption had largely returned to what was regarded as normal. But a strong sense of crisis remained, not least because the oil boycott was a perfect illustration of the fact that the American economy and way of life were heavily dependent on limited natural resources (limits being imposed by political machinations or by nature itself) and could easily be disrupted, even brought to a standstill. This in turn was tied in with debates (outlined in the Introduction) about, and indeed in many cases the direct experience of, stagflation, social unrest and governmental dysfunction in the USA, worldwide population growth and unsustainable consumption levels, global environmental destruction and international conflict.

American Graffiti took audiences back to a time when the future looked much brighter. When asked to rate the state of the country on a scale from 1 to 10, in 1959 and 1964 survey responses had averaged out at 6.7 and 6.5, respectively, with the past ('5 Years Ago') judged to have been worse and the future ('5 Years from Now') expected to be much better (Ladd and Bowman 1998: 45–6). Several surveys from the years 1971 to 1974 found that at this point the present was rated between 5.4 and 4.3, a roughly 20–30% drop from 1959/64. Respondents felt that things had got worse in the preceding five years, but there still was an expectation of improvements across the next five years. However, the expected rating in five years was between 6.2 and 5.4, as compared to 7.4/7.7 as expected in the 1959/64 surveys. After ratings of both the present and the future had gone down from 1971 to 1974, there was a slight overall improvement thereafter, and yet for the rest of the 70s (and indeed beyond) ratings did not reach the results at the beginning of the decade, let alone those from 1959/64.

American Graffiti made its biggest impact in 1973/74, at the low point of this development. As discussed in Chapter 3, reviewers – and presumably the film's general audience, mostly made up of educated baby boomers – perceived *American Graffiti* not just as a celebration of an earlier period in American history and an exciting stage in people's lives, but also as a story about the limitations of teenage existence and the inevitability of personal and societal change. The oil crisis brought into focus many of the developments that Americans had every reason to worry and be rather pessimistic about. Such worry and pessimism in turn encouraged a nostalgic turn to the past, not just to escape the present, but to gain a fresh perspective on it, perhaps even to identify some of the historical roots of current problems, and as a reminder of the fact that challenges had been met successfully in the past and of the social cohesion that had made this possible.

One of the insights offered by *American Graffiti* was that material possessions and paid-for goods and services are so much less important than human connections and social relationships. This tied in nicely with one of the key lessons to be learnt from the intense debates of the late 1960s and early 1970s about the economy, population growth and environmentalism, namely, that a consumerist lifestyle is unsustainable. But in hindsight it is obvious that baby boomers (and Americans more generally) were not inclined to reduce the high consumption levels they had gotten used to since the 1950s. To be sure, many of them were critical of established institutions and ways of life, but most were already thoroughly hooked on a consumerist lifestyle. What is more, this lifestyle became an aspirational model for people all around the world. *American Graffiti* did not make a big impact outside the United States, but the kind of postwar consumerism it depicted (and, I have argued, critiqued) surely did.

Notes

1 This paragraph and the next two are mainly based on Perlstein (2014: 111–3, 184–5, 196–8, 211, 220), Leggett (2006: 26, 142–8) and Frum (2000: 314–22).

2 Cp. Andreas Killen's (2007: 177–85) discussion of *American Graffiti* in relation to the oil crisis. Killen sees the film merely as an escape from the present and does not acknowledge that it also offers a critique of the past. Similarly, in a survey article relating films to various stages of 'automobile consciousness' in the United States, Ken Hey (1976: 27) associates *American Graffiti* with 'mass idolization' of cars rather than a later, critical stage.

Bibliography

'All-Time Box Office Champs' (1973) *Variety*, 3 January, p. 30.

'All-Time Film Rental Champs' (1976) *Variety*, 7 January, p. 20.

'All-Time Film Rental Champs' (1977) *Variety*, 5 January, p. 16.

Alpert, H. (1973) *'American Graffiti,' New York World*, 14 August, p. 41.

Altschuler, G.C. (2003) *All Shook Up: How Rock 'n' Roll Changed America*, Oxford: Oxford University Press.

'American Graffiti' (1973) *New York Times*, 19 August, p. D12.

Bailey, B. (1994) 'Sexual Revolution(s),' in D. Farber (ed) *The Sixties: From Memory to History*, Chapel Hill: University of North Carolina Press, pp. 235–62.

Baxter, J. (1999) *George Lucas: A Biography*, New York, NY: HarperCollins.

Beck, J. (2016) *Designing Sound: Audiovisual Aesthetics in 1970s American Cinema*, New Brunswick, NJ: Rutgers University Press.

Berliner, T. (2010) *Hollywood Incoherent: Narration in Seventies Cinema*, Austin: University of Texas Press.

'Big Rental Films of 1971' (1972) *Variety*, 5 January, p. 9.

'Big Rental Films of 1972' (1973) *Variety*, 3 January, p. 7.

'Big Rental Films of 1973' (1974) *Variety*, 9 January, p. 19.

Block, A.B. and Wilson, L.A. (eds) (2010) *George Lucas's Blockbusting: A Decade-by-Decade Survey of Timeless Movies Including Untold Secrets of Their Financial and Cultural Success*, New York, NY: itbooks.

Breines, W. (1992) *Young, White, and Miserable: Growing Up Female in the Fifties*, Chicago, IL: University of Chicago Press.

Brickman, B.J. (2014) *New American Teenagers: The Lost Generation of Youth in 1970s Film*, New York, NY: Bloomsbury Academic.

Brode, D. (2015) *Sex, Drugs & Rock 'n' Roll: The Evolution of an American Youth Culture*, New York, NY: Peter Lang.

Brooks, V.D. (2009) *Boomers: The Cold-War Generation Grows Up*, Chicago, IL: Ivan R. Dee.

Bryant, F.B., Smart, C.M. and King, S.P. (2005) 'Using the Past to Enhance the Present: Boosting Happiness Through Positive Reminiscence,' *Journal of Happiness Studies*, No. 6, pp. 227–60.

Cader, M. (2000) *2001 People Entertainment Almanac*, New York, NY: Cader Books.

Canby, V. (1973) '*American Graffiti* and *Heavy Traffic,*' *New York Times*, 16 September, p. D1.

Carroll, K. (1973) '*American Graffiti*: Funny, Poignant Film,' *New York Daily News*, 13 August, p. 45.

Chis, C. (1973) '*American Graffiti,*' *New York*, 13 August, p. 60.

Cocks, J. (1973) 'Fabulous '50s,' *Time*, 20 August, p. 58.

Cohen, L. (2003) *A Consumers' Republic: The Politics of Mass Consumption in Postwar America*, New York, NY: Vintage.

Colby, S.L. and Ortman, J.M. (2014) 'The Baby Boom Cohort in the United States: 2012 to 2060,' US Census Bureau, https://www.census.gov/prod/2014pubs/p25-1141.pdf.

Coleman, J.S. (1961) *The Adolescent Society: The Social Life of the Teenager and Its Impact on Education*, New York, NY: The Free Press.

Cook, D.A. (2000) *Lost Illusions: American Cinema in the Shadow of Watergate and Vietnam, 1970–1979*, New York, NY: Scribner's.

Cooper, B.L. (1974) Review of *41 Original Hits From the Soundtrack of American Graffiti'*, *The History Teacher*, Vol. 7, No. 2, February, pp. 283–4.

Cross, G. (2015) *Consumed Nostalgia: Memory in the Age of Fast Capitalism*, New York, NY: Columbia University Press.

Cross, G.S. (2018) *Machines of Youth: America's Car Obsession*, Chicago, IL: University of Chicago Press.

Curtis, J.M. (1980) 'From *American Graffiti* to *Star Wars,*' *Journal of Popular Culture*, Vol. 13, No. 4, Spring, pp. 590–601.

Dallas, L. (2015) 'It's a Richard Walter World,' *Creative Screenwriting*, online, 18 August, https://creativescreenwriting.com/its-a-richard-walter-world/.

Dawson, J. (2005) Rock Around the Clock: *The Record That Started the Rock Revolution*, San Francisco, CA: Backbeat Books.

Decker, M.T. (2009) 'They Want Unfreedom and One-Dimensional Thought? I'll Give Them Unfreedom and One-Dimensional Thought: George Lucas, *THX-1138*, and the Persistence of Marcusian Social Critique in *American Graffiti* and the *Star Wars* Films,' *Extrapolation*, Vol. 50, No. 3, pp. 417–41.

Decker, M.T. (2016) *Industrial Society and the Science Fiction Blockbuster: Social Critique in Films of Lucas, Scott and Cameron*, Jefferson, NC: McFarland.

Dempsey, M. (1973) Review of *American Graffiti*, *Film Quarterly*, Vol. 27, No. 1, Autumn, pp. 58–60.

Dennis, J.P. (2008) *Queering Teen Culture: All-American Boys and Same-Sex Desire in Film and Television*, New York, NY: Routledge.

DeWitt, J. (2010) 'Cars and Culture: The Cars of *American Graffiti,*' *The American Poetry Review*, Vol. 39, No. 5, September-October, pp. 47–50.

Dick, B.F. (1997) *City of Dreams: The Making and Remaking of Universal Pictures*. Lexington: University of Kentucky Press.

Dika, V. (2003) *Recycled Culture in Contemporary Art and Film: The Uses of Nostalgia*, Cambridge: Cambridge University Press.

Doherty, T. (1988) *Teenagers & Teenpics: The Juvenilization of American Movies in the 1950s*, Boston, MA: Unwin Hyman.

Douglas, S.J. (1995) *Where the Girls Are: Growing Up Female with the Mass Media*, London: Penguin.

Dwyer, M.D. (2015) *Back to the Fifties: Nostalgia, Hollywood Film, and Popular Music of the Seventies and Eighties*, New York, NY: Oxford University Press.

Ebert, R. (1973) 'American Graffiti,' *Chicago Sun-Times*, online, 11 August, https://www.rogerebert.com/reviews/american-graffiti-1973.

Erskine, H. (1972) 'The Polls: Pollution and Its Costs,' *Public Opinion Quarterly*, Vol. 36, No. 1, pp. 120–35.

Fairchild, B.H. (1979) 'Songs of Innocence and Experience: The Blakean Vision of George Lucas,' *Literature/Film Quarterly*, Vol. 7, No. 2, pp. 112–9.

Farber, S. (1973) 'Graffiti Ranks with Bonnie and Clyde,' *New York Times*, 5 August, pp. D1, D6.

Farber, S. (1974) 'George Lucas: The Stinky Kid Hits the Big Time,' *Film Quarterly*, Vol. 27, No. 3, Spring, pp. 2–9, reprinted in S. Kline (ed) (1999) *George Lucas: Interviews*, Jackson: University Press of Mississippi, pp. 33–44.

Finler, J.W. (1988) *The Hollywood Story*, London: Octopus.

Frank, E. (1973) 'Movies,' *Ann Arbor Sun*, 24 September, p. 15.

Frum, D. (2000) *How We Got Here: The 70s*, New York, NY: Basic Books.

Gardner, P. (1973) 'Graffiti Reflects Its Director's Youth,' *New York Times*, 19 September, p. D40.

Genauer, E. (1973) 'American Graffiti,' *New York Post*, 8 September, p. 34.

Gilbert, J. (1986) *A Cycle of Outrage: America's Reaction to the Juvenile Delinquent in the 1950s*, New York, NY: Oxford University Press.

Gilliatt, P. (1973) 'American Graffiti,' *New Yorker*, 13 August, p. 66.

Gillon, S. (2004) *Boomer Nation: The Largest and Richest Generation Ever and How It Changed America*. New York, NY: Free Press.

Godfrey, N. (2014) 'Reading American Graffiti,' *Screen Education*, Vol. 74, Winter, pp. 118–23.

Godfrey, N. (2018) *The Limits of Auteurism: Case Studies in the Critically Constructed New Hollywood*, New Brunswick, NJ: Rutgers University Press.

Greenspun, R. (1973) 'California Elegy: American Graffiti Has Premiere at Sutton,' *New York Times*, 13 August, p. D21.

Gruner, O. (2016) *Screening the Sixties: Hollywood Cinema and the Politics of Memory*, London: Palgrave Macmillan.

Gruner, O. and Krämer, P. (eds) (2020) *'Grease is the Word': Exploring a Cultural Phenomenon*, London: Anthem.

Hall, M.K. (2014) *The Emergence of Rock and Roll: Music and the Rise of American Youth Culture*, New York, NY: Routledge.

Hall, S. and Neale, S. (2010) *Epics, Spectacles and Blockbusters: A Hollywood History*, Detroit, MI: Wayne State University Press.

Harmetz, A. (1983) 'Burden of Dreams: George Lucas,' *American Film*, June, pp. 30–35, reprinted in S. Kline (ed) (1999) *George Lucas: Interviews*, Jackson: University Press of Mississippi, pp. 135–44.

Haskell, M. (1973) 'Movies 1973,' *The Massachusetts Review*, Vol. 14, No. 4, Autumn, pp. 815–33.

Hearn, M. (2005) *The Cinema of George Lucas*, New York, NY: Harry N. Abrams.

Herman, F. (1973) '*American Graffiti*,' *Modesto Bee*, 13 September, unpaginated clipping from Richard Ravalli's personal collection.

Hey, K. (1976) '"Some Day This will All Be Ours": Automobile Consciousness and the American Film,' *Film & History*, Vol. 6, No. 2, May, pp. 25–30, 40–1.

Howard, A.R. (1973) 'Graffiti Survived Studios' Rejection to Score at B.O.,' *Hollywood Reporter*, online, 24 August, https:/www.hollywoodreporter. com/news/american-graffiti-making-george-lucas-film-1130166.

Howe, N. and Strauss, W. (2000) *Millennials Rising: The Next Great Generation*, New York, NY: Vintage.

Huff, W.K.K. (2011) 'Wolfman Jack (Robert Smith), 1938–1995,' in C.H. Sterling (ed) *The Biographical Encyclopedia of American Radio*, New York, NY: Routledge, 416–7.

Jack, W. with Laursen, B. (1995) *Have Mercy! Confessions of the Original Rock 'n' Roll Animal*, New York, NY: Warner Books.

James, D.E. (2017) *Rock 'n' Film: Cinema's Dance with Popular Music*, New York, NY: Oxford University Press.

Jameson, F. (1984) 'Postmodernism, or The Cultural Logic of Late Capitalism,' *New Left Review*, No. 146, pp. 52–92.

Jenkins, G. (1998) *Empire Building: The Remarkable Real Life Story of Star Wars*, New York, NY: Simon and Schuster.

Jones, B.J. (2016) *George Lucas: A Life*, London: Headline.

Jones, L.Y. (1980) *Great Expectations: America and the Baby Boom Generation*, New York, NY: Coward, McCann & Geoghegan.

Kael, P. (1973) '*American Graffiti*,' *New Yorker*, 29 October, p. 154.

Kaminski, M. (2008) *The Secret History of* Star Wars*: The Art of Storytelling and the Making of a Modern Epic*, Kingston, Ontario: Legacy.

Kanfer, S. (1967) 'The Shock of Freedom in Films,' *Time*, 8 December, pp. 66–76, reprinted in A.F. McClure (ed) (1971) *The Movies: An American Idiom*, Rutherford, NJ: Fairleigh Dickinson University Press, pp. 322–33.

Killen, A. (2007) *1973 Nervous Breakdown: Watergate, Warhol, and the Birth of Post-Sixties America*, New York, NY: Bloomsbury.

Kissel, H. (1973) '*American Graffiti*,' *Women's Wear Daily*, 13 August, p. 18.

Klein, A.A. (2011) *American Film Cycles: Reframing Genres, Screening Social Problems and Defining Subcultures*, Austin: University of Texas Press.

Klemesrud, J. (1973) '*Graffiti* is the Story of His Life,' *New York Times*, 7 October, pp. D1, 13.

Krämer, P. (1998) 'Post-classical Hollywood,' in J. Hill and P. Church Gibson (eds) *The Oxford Guide to Film Studies*, Oxford: Oxford University Press, pp. 289–309.

Krämer, P. (1999) 'A Powerful Cinema-going Force? Hollywood and Female Audiences since the 1960s,' in M. Stokes and R. Maltby (eds) *Identifying Hollywood's Audiences: Cultural Identity and the Movies*, London: BFI, pp. 98–112.

Krämer, P. (2005) *The New Hollywood: From Bonnie and Clyde to Star Wars*, London: Wallflower Press.

Krämer, P. (2008/2018) '"Where were you in '62?" *American Graffiti*, George Lucas and the Baby Boom Generation', manuscript of talk presented at 'A Modesto Celebration of the 35th Anniversary of George Lucas' *American Graffiti*,' Modesto, California, 31 May 2008; posted on Kip's American Graffiti Blog, 2 August 2018, http://kipsamericangraffiti.blogspot.com/2018/08/.

Krämer, P. (2014) *Dr. Strangelove or: How I Learned to Stop Worrying and Love the Bomb*, London: British Film Institute.

Krämer, P. (2020) '"An Easy Winner": The Marketing, Reception and Success of *Grease*,' in O. Gruner and P. Krämer (eds) *'Grease is the Word': Exploring a Cultural Phenomenon*, London: Anthem, pp. 145–63.

Krämer, P. (2022) '"One More Fine Technician for the Dream Factory"? George Lucas's Early Film Career, 1964–1971,' *Film History*, Vol. 34, No. 2, pp. 35–62.

Krämer, P. and Tzioumakis, Y. (2018) 'Introduction,' in P. Krämer and Y. Tzioumakis (eds) *The Hollywood Renaissance: Revisiting American Cinema's Most Celebrated Era*, New York, NY: Bloomsbury Academic, pp. xiii–xxvii.

Ladd, E.C. and Bowman, K.H (1998) *What's Wrong: A Survey of American Satisfaction and Complaint*, Washington, D.C.: The AEI Press.

Langford, B. (2007) *'American Graffiti* (1973),' in M. Merck (ed) *America First: Naming the Nation in US Film*, London: Routledge, pp. 157–76.

Leggett, J. (2006) *Half Gone: Oil, Gas, Hot Air and the Global Energy Crisis*, London: Portobello.

Le Sueur, M. (1977) 'Theory Number Five: Anatomy of Nostalgia Films: Heritage and Methods,' *Journal of Popular Film*, Vol. 6, No. 2, January, pp. 187–97.

Lewis, J. (1995) *Whom God Wishes to Destroy...: Francis Coppola and the New Hollywood*, Durham, NC: Duke University Press.

Light, P.C. (1988) *Baby Boomers*, New York, NY: W.W. Norton.

Lucas, G., Katz, G. and Huyck, H. (1973) *American Graffiti: A Screenplay*, New York, NY: Grove.

Lucas, G., Katz, G. and Huyck, W. (1972) *American Graffiti* screenplay, 'second draft', dated 10 May, https://cinephiliabeyond.org/wp-content/uploads/2015/08/American-Graffiti.pdf?x91765.

MacKinnon, K. (1984) *Hollywood's Small Towns: An Introduction to the American Small-Town Movie*, Metuchen: Scarecrow.

Marcus, D. (2004) *Happy Days and Wonder Years: The Fifties and Sixties in Contemporary Cultural Politics*, New Brunswick, NJ: Rutgers University Press.

Marez, C. (2016) *Farm Worker Futurism: Speculative Technologies of Resistance*, Minneapolis: University of Minnesota Press.

Marshall, G., with Marshall, L. (1995) *Wake Me When It's Funny: How to Break into Show Business and Stay There*, New York, NY: Newmarket Press.

McCarthy, P. (2014) *The Lucas Effect: George Lucas and the New Hollywood*, Youngstown, OH: Teneo Press.

McGee, M.T. and Robertson, R.J. (1982) *The J.D. Films: Juvenile Delinquency in the Movies*, Jefferson, NC: McFarland.

Medovoi, L. (2005) *Rebels: Youth and the Cold War Origins of Identity*, Durham, NC: Duke University Press.

Milius, J. (1969) *Apocalypse Now* screenplay, 'first draft', 5 December, own collection.

Minahan, J. (1979) *The Complete American Graffiti: The Novel*, London: Magnum.

Murphy, A.D. (1973) *'American Graffiti,' Variety*, 20 June, p. 20.

Murray, J.P. (1973) 'Reel Images – The Film Scene,' *New York Amsterdam News*, 25 August, p. D5.

Nash, I. (2006) *American Sweethearts: Teenage Girls in Twentieth-Century Popular Culture*, Bloomington: Indiana University Press.

National Council of Churches (1973) *Film Information: A Source of the Broadcasting and Film Commission*, September.

Neumann, W.R. (1990) 'The Threshold of Public Attention,' *Public Opinion Quarterly*, Vol. 54, pp. 159–76.

Noble, G. (1983) 'Social Learning from Everyday Television,' in M.J.A. Howe (ed) *Learning from Television: Psychological and Educational Research*, London: Academic Press, pp. 101–24.

'N.Y. Critics' Opinions' (1973) *Variety*, 15 August, p. 7.

Ondaatje, M. (2002) *The Conversations: Walter Murch and the Art of Editing Film*, London: Bloomsbury.

Palladino, G. (1996) *Teenagers: An American History*, New York, NY: BasicBooks.

Perlstein, R. (2015) *The Invisible Bridge: The Fall of Nixon and the Rise of Reagan*, New York, NY: Simon & Schuster.

Petigny, A. (2009) *The Permissive Society: America, 1941–1965*, Cambridge: Cambridge University Press.

Phillips, M. (2009) *High on Arrival: A Memoir*, New York, NY: Gallery Books.

Pollock, D. (1990) *Skywalking: The Life and Films of George Lucas*, Hollywood, CA: Samuel French.

'Population Profile Favors Pix' (1975) *Variety*, 3 October, pp. 1, 3–4.

Pye, M. and Myles, L. (1979) *The Movie Brats: How the Film School Generation Took Over Hollywood*, New York, NY: Holt, Rinehart and Winston.

Ravalli, R. (2007) '"From a Place Not Far, Far Away": The Modesto Years of George Lucas, Jr.,' *Stanislaus Stepping Stones: The Bimonthly Journal of the McHenry Museum & Historical Society*, September-October, pp. 1697–701.

Reed, R. (1973) *'American Graffiti,' New York Daily News*, 5 August, p. 5.

Rinzler, J.W. (2007) *The Making of Star Wars: The Definitive Story Behind the Original Film*, New York, NY: Ballantine.

Robertson, T. (2012) *The Malthusian Moment: Global Population Growth and the Birth of American Environmentalism*, New Brunswick, NJ: Rutgers University Press.

Rossi, U. (2009) 'Acousmatic Presences: From DJs to Talk-Radio Hosts in American Fiction, Cinema, and Drama,' *Mosaic*, Vol. 42, No. 1, March, pp. 83–98.

Rowlands, P. (2012) 'Candy Clark Talks About *American Graffiti*,' *Money Into Light*, online, http://www.money-into-light.com/2012/04/candy-clark-talks-to-paul-rowlands.html.

Rubin, M. (2006) *Droidmaker: George Lucas and the Digital Revolution*, Gainesville, FL: Triad.

Russell, J. and Whalley, J. (2018) *Hollywood and the Baby Boom: A Social History*, New York, NY: Bloomsbury Academic.

Schumacher, M. (2000) *Francis Ford Coppola: A Filmmaker's Life*, London: Bloomsbury.

Schuman, H. and Scott, J. (1989) 'Generations and Collective Memories,' *American Sociological Review*, Vol. 54, June, pp. 359–81.

Shumway, D.R. (1999) 'Rock'n'Roll Sound Tracks and the Production of Nostalgia,' *Cinema Journal*, Vol. 38, No. 2, Winter, pp. 36–51.

Smith, F. (2017) *Rethinking the Hollywood Teen Movie: Gender, Genre and Identity*, Edinburgh: Edinburgh University Press.

Smith, F. (2018) 'Smoke Gets in Your Eyes: Re-Reading Gender in the "Nostalgia Film",' *Quarterly Review of Film and Video*, Vol. 35, No. 5, pp. 463–87.

Smith, J. (1998) *The Sounds of Commerce: Marketing Popular Film Music*, New York, NY: Columbia University Press.

Smith, J. (2003) *George Lucas*, London: Virgin.

Smith, T. (1980) 'America's Most Important Problem – A Trend Analysis, 1946–1976,' *Public Opinion Quarterly*, Vol. 44, No. 2, Summer, pp. 164–80.

Smith, T. (1985) 'The Polls: America's Most Important Problems Part I: National and International,' *Public Opinion Quarterly*, Vol. 49, No. 2, Summer, pp. 264–74.

Sodowsky, A., Sodowsky, R. and Witte, S. (1975) 'The Epic World of *American Graffiti*,' *Journal of Popular Film*, Vol. 4, No. 1, January, pp. 47–55.

Speed, L. (1998) 'Tuesday's Gone: The Nostalgic Teen Film,' *Journal of Popular Film and Television*, Vol. 26, No. 1, pp. 24–32.

Sprengler, C. (2009) *Screening Nostalgia: Populuxe Props and Technicolor Aesthetics in Contemporary American Film*, New York, NY: Berghahn.

Staiger, J. (2000) *Blockbuster TV: Must-See Sitcoms in the Network Era*, New York, NY: New York University Press.

Stanley Bare, C. (1999) *Modesto Then and Now*, Modesto, CA: McHenry Museum Press.

Steinberg, C. (1980) *Film Facts*, New York, NY: Facts on File.

Steinhorn, L. (2006) *The Greater Generation: In Defense of the Baby Boom Legacy*, New York, NY: Thomas Dunne Books.

Stempel, T. (2001) *American Audiences on Movies and Moviegoing*, Lexington: University Press of Kentucky.

Stone, J. (1971) 'George Lucas,' *San Francisco Chronicle*, 23 May, reprinted in S. Kline (ed) (1999) *George Lucas: Interviews*, Jackson: University Press of Mississippi, pp. 3–7.

Sturhahn, L. (1974) 'The Filming of *American Graffiti*,' *Filmmakers Newsletter*, March, pp. 19–27, reprinted in S. Kline (ed) (1999) *George Lucas: Interviews*, Jackson: University Press of Mississippi, pp. 14–32.

Sweeney, L. (1973) 'Only 1962 and Already Nostalgia?,' *Christian Science Monitor*, 20 August, p. 14.

Symmons, T. (2016) *The New Hollywood Historical Film, 1967–78*, London: Palgrave Macmillan.

Tannenwald, N. (2007) *The Nuclear Taboo: The United States and the Non-Use of Nuclear Weapons Since 1945*, Cambridge: Cambridge University Press.

Taylor, C. (2016) *How Star Wars Conquered the Universe*, London: Head of Zeus.

'The Brakes' (1973) *Village Voice*, 23 August, p. 75.

'The Class of 1974' (1974) *America's Miss Junior Pageant*, p. 57.

Tropiano, S. (2006) *Rebels & Chicks: A History of the Hollywood Teen Movie*, New York, NY: Back Stage Books.

Universal (1973) Press Book for *American Graffiti*, *American Graffiti* clippings file, Billy Rose Theatre Collection, New York Public Library at Lincoln Center, New York.

'Updated All-Time Film Champs' (1974) *Variety*, 9 January, p. 23.

'Updated All-Time Film Champs' (1975) *Variety*, 8 January, p. 26.

Vallely, J. (1980) '*The Empire Strikes Back* and So Does Filmmaker George Lucas with his Sequel to *Star Wars*,' *Rolling Stone*, 12 June, pp. 31–3, reprinted in S. Kline (ed) (1999) *George Lucas: Interviews*, Jackson: University Press of Mississippi, pp. 87–97.

Veroff, J., Douvan, E. and Kulka, R.A. (1981) *The Inner American: A Self-Portrait from 1957 to 1976*, New York: Basic Books.

Verrill, A. (1971) 'Youth Shuns Youth-Lure Films: 74% of Patrons but They Stray,' *Variety*, 3 November, p. 1.

Wall, T. and Webber, N. (2020) 'Rock 'n' Roll: Cars, Convergence and Culture,' in M. Duffett and P. Beate (eds) *Popular Music and Automobiles*, New York, NY: Bloomsbury Academic, pp. 15–32.

Warren, M. and Levine, R.A. (1975) 'New Hollywood: Gloria Katz-Willard Huyck Interview,' *Film Comment*, Vol. 11, No. 2, March-April, pp. 47–53.

Wattenberg, B.J. (ed) (1976) *The Statistical History of the United States*, New York, NY: Basic Books.

Wildschut, T., Sedikides, C., Routledge, C. and Arndt, J. (2006) 'Nostalgia: Content, Triggers, Functions,' *Journal of Personality and Social Psychology*, Vol. 91, No. 5, pp. 975–93.

Winsten, A. (1973) '*American Graffiti* Opens,' *New York Post*, 13 August, p. 21.

'Young Directors, New Films' (1973) *AFI Report*, Winter, pp. 45–6.

Zimmerman, P.D. (1973) 'Drag-Strip Dance,' *Newsweek*, 13 August, p. 93.

Index

Note: Page numbers followed by "n" denote endnotes.